Quantum Computing for Beginners

Understanding the Next Tech Revolution How quantum computers work and why they matter

THOMPSON CARTER

Table of Content

TABLE OF CONTENTS

INTRODUCTION

The dawn of quantum computing is upon us, and it promises to transform industries, solve complex problems, and revolutionize the way we process information. As technology continues to evolve, we are approaching a time when **quantum computers** will no longer be just an academic concept but will become central to solving real-world challenges that classical computers have struggled with for decades. From healthcare and cryptography to artificial intelligence and climate modeling, quantum computing holds the potential to change the world as we know it.

But what exactly is quantum computing, and how does it differ from the traditional computing systems we use today? How does it work, and what makes it so powerful? This book, **Quantum Computing for Beginners: Understanding the Next Tech Revolution**, is designed to answer these questions and more, providing you with a comprehensive introduction to the fascinating world of quantum computing.

In the chapters that follow, we will explore the **fundamentals of quantum mechanics**, which form the backbone of quantum computing. We will explain key concepts like **qubits**, **superposition**, **entanglement**, and **quantum interference**, and show how these principles allow quantum computers to perform calculations that classical computers simply cannot. By drawing on real-world examples, we will demonstrate how quantum computing could transform industries such as **medicine, finance, cryptography**, and **cloud computing**.

Why Quantum Computing Matters

The advent of quantum computing presents a **paradigm shift** in computational power. While classical computers, which rely on bits to represent data as 0s and 1s, have served humanity well for decades, they are reaching the limits of their capabilities when it comes to solving certain problems. For example, problems involving **large-scale optimization, complex simulations**, or **machine learning** can take classical computers years to solve, even with the most powerful supercomputers in existence.

Quantum computers, on the other hand, leverage the strange and counterintuitive properties of quantum mechanics to perform these tasks in a fraction of the time. By harnessing **quantum bits (qubits)**, quantum computers can represent and process information in ways that classical computers cannot. They can analyze vast amounts of data simultaneously, enabling faster, more efficient solutions to problems in areas ranging from **drug discovery** and **material science** to **cryptography** and **cybersecurity**.

Who This Book Is For

This book is intended for anyone interested in understanding **quantum computing**, regardless of their technical background. Whether you're a **student**, a **professional in a related field**, or simply a **curious reader** eager to understand the future of computing, this book provides a solid foundation in quantum computing principles.

For beginners, we break down complex concepts into easy-to-understand explanations, guiding you step by step through the core ideas that underpin quantum technologies. **Real-world examples**, **analogies**, and **visual aids** will help simplify these abstract ideas and demonstrate their practical applications.

For those with a background in computer science, physics, or engineering, the book offers deeper insights into the mathematical and theoretical aspects of quantum computing, and it introduces you to **quantum algorithms**, programming languages like **Qiskit**, and the latest developments in **quantum hardware**.

What You Will Learn

Through this book, you will:

- **Understand the Basics of Quantum Mechanics**: Learn about the strange phenomena of quantum mechanics, including **superposition**, **entanglement**, and **quantum**

interference, and how they form the basis for quantum computing.

- **Explore Quantum Algorithms**: Discover how algorithms like **Shor's Algorithm** and **Grover's Algorithm** are designed to harness the power of quantum computing to solve problems much faster than classical algorithms.

- **Dive into Quantum Hardware**: Get an overview of the **different types of quantum computers**, including **superconducting qubits, trapped ions**, and **quantum annealing**, and understand the challenges of building quantum computers.

- **Learn How Quantum Computing Will Impact Industries**: Explore the potential applications of quantum computing in fields like **cryptography, medicine, finance, cloud computing**, and **artificial intelligence**.

- **Get Practical with Quantum Programming**: Learn how to start writing quantum programs using tools like **IBM Q Experience** and **Qiskit**, and run basic quantum algorithms on real quantum processors.

Structure of the Book

The book is divided into **27 chapters**, each focusing on a different aspect of quantum computing:

1. **Introduction to Quantum Computing**: What quantum computing is and why it matters.

2. **The Basics of Classical Computing**: Understanding how classical computers work and the limitations that quantum computing addresses.

3. **The Principles of Quantum Mechanics**: Key quantum concepts such as superposition and entanglement.

4. **Qubits – The Building Blocks of Quantum Computers**: How qubits represent data and why they're different from classical bits.

5. **Superposition – More Than Just a 1 or 0**: Understanding superposition and its implications for quantum computing.

6. **Entanglement – Spooky Action at a Distance**: How entanglement works and its applications.

7. **Quantum Interference – Using Probability to Your Advantage**: How quantum interference optimizes calculations.

8. **Quantum Gates and Circuits**: An introduction to quantum gates and how they manipulate qubits.

9. **Quantum Algorithms**: An overview of quantum algorithms and their potential speedups.

10. **Shor's Algorithm and Cryptography**: How quantum computers can break RSA encryption.

11. **Grover's Algorithm and Search Optimization**: How quantum computers can speed up search problems.

12. **Quantum Speedup**: The potential for quantum computers to solve problems faster than classical systems.

13. **Quantum Decoherence – The Quantum Challenge**: The problem of quantum decoherence and how it affects quantum systems.

14. **Quantum Error Correction**: Techniques for making quantum computers reliable.

15. **Quantum Hardware**: The physical realization of quantum computers and the challenges involved.

16. **Quantum Programming Languages**: How to write quantum programs using languages like Qiskit.

17. **Quantum Simulations**: Using quantum computers for simulations in fields like drug discovery and material science.

18. **Quantum Communication and Networks**: How quantum communication can secure data transmission.

19. **The Quantum Internet**: How quantum computing will revolutionize the internet and global communication.

20. **Quantum Computing for Machine Learning**: How quantum computing can accelerate AI and machine learning.

21. **Quantum Computing and Artificial Intelligence**: The synergies between quantum computing and AI.

22. **Quantum Computing in Healthcare and Drug Discovery**: How quantum computing is transforming medicine.

Why This Book Matters

As we stand at the precipice of the quantum computing revolution, it is essential to understand both the potential benefits and the challenges that lie ahead. Quantum computing will change how we approach complex problems and create solutions that we cannot yet fully imagine. By understanding the fundamentals of quantum computing and the potential impact it will have on various industries, you will be better prepared to engage with the technology, whether you're pursuing a career in tech, research, or simply exploring new frontiers in science.

This book aims to be your guide to the world of quantum computing, offering a thorough yet accessible introduction to the subject. Whether you're a complete beginner or a seasoned professional, it provides the knowledge and tools to help you understand and embrace the **quantum future**.

Let's embark on this journey into the **quantum revolution**!

CHAPTER 1

WHAT IS QUANTUM COMPUTING?

Quantum computing is an emerging field in technology that promises to revolutionize how we solve complex problems. But before we dive into the intricacies of quantum computers, it's important to first understand what traditional or classical computing is, and how quantum computing stands apart.

Classical Computing: The Basics

At the core of classical computing, you'll find something known as **bits**. A bit is the smallest unit of data in a classical computer and can be in one of two possible states: **0** or **1**. Every task that a classical computer performs—whether it's running an application, playing a video, or browsing the web—relies on the manipulation of these bits.

For example, when you click on a link in a browser, the computer processes this click by transforming it into a series of binary instructions (0s and 1s), which tell the computer how to display the page. Classical computers follow a straightforward approach to solving problems: they process each instruction step-by-step.

14

Quantum Computing: The Basics

Quantum computing, however, operates on a different level entirely. Instead of **bits**, quantum computers use **qubits** (quantum bits). Unlike classical bits, qubits can represent not just **0** or **1**, but both values simultaneously, thanks to a property known as **superposition**. This means that a quantum computer can process multiple possibilities at the same time, exponentially increasing its potential to solve certain types of problems.

Let's break it down further:

- **Classical computers** use bits, which are binary and can either be 0 or 1.
- **Quantum computers** use qubits, which can exist in multiple states at once, thanks to quantum mechanics. They can be 0, 1, or both at the same time (superposition).

Real-World Example: Classical vs. Quantum

Imagine you're at a crossroads, and you have two paths ahead. A classical computer would decide which path to take and move forward, one step at a time. But a quantum computer, thanks to superposition, could explore both paths simultaneously, figuring out the best route in one go.

Here's another example: Imagine you're searching through a massive library with millions of books, trying to find a specific one. A classical computer would check each book, one by one, whereas a quantum computer could examine multiple books simultaneously, drastically speeding up the process.

Why Does This Matter?

The advantage of quantum computing lies in its ability to perform parallel processing on a massive scale. Certain problems, like simulating molecular structures for drug discovery, optimizing large-scale systems, or factoring large numbers (important in cryptography), are practically impossible for classical computers to solve efficiently. Quantum computers, however, could potentially solve these problems in a fraction of the time.

Key Differences Between Classical and Quantum Computing:

Aspect	Classical Computing	Quantum Computing
Basic Unit	Bit (0 or 1)	Qubit (0, 1, or both simultaneously due to superposition)

Aspect	Classical Computing	Quantum Computing
Processing	Sequential: One calculation after another	Parallel: Multiple calculations at once, thanks to superposition
Problem Solving	Solves problems step-by-step	Solves certain problems exponentially faster using quantum phenomena like entanglement
Suitability	Ideal for general-purpose tasks and everyday computing	Ideal for specific complex problems like cryptography, optimization, and simulations
Power	Limited by Moore's Law (traditional scaling)	Potential for massive parallelism, possibly breaking current computational limits

Why Does Quantum Computing Matter?

Classical computers have served us well for decades. However, as problems grow increasingly complex, classical computing reaches its limits. Quantum computing opens the door to **next-generation solutions**, potentially enabling breakthroughs in areas like:

- **Medicine**: Developing drugs and treatments by simulating molecular structures.
- **Cryptography**: Strengthening cybersecurity or breaking existing encryption methods.
- **Artificial Intelligence**: Speeding up machine learning algorithms and enhancing data analysis.
- **Optimization**: Improving efficiency in logistics, traffic management, and supply chains.

By enabling faster, more efficient computations, quantum computers could lead to revolutionary advancements across various fields. As we continue to explore this technology, it is clear that quantum computing has the potential to change the world in ways we are only beginning to understand.

In this chapter, we've set the stage for what quantum computing is, how it differs from classical computing, and why it's such an exciting and transformative field. In the following chapters, we'll dive deeper into the principles that make quantum computing possible, its underlying science, and how these ideas are being practically applied in the real world.

CHAPTER 2

THE BASICS OF CLASSICAL COMPUTING

Before we delve into quantum computing, it's essential to understand how classical computers work. Classical computing forms the backbone of the technology we use every day, from smartphones to laptops to the servers that power the internet. In this chapter, we will break down the fundamental components of classical computing, using real-world examples to illustrate how it solves problems, and highlight the limitations that quantum computing is designed to address.

How Classical Computers Solve Problems:

At the heart of every classical computer lies a process called **binary computation**, which uses **binary code** (a system of 1s and 0s) to represent and manipulate data. Let's explore how this works.

1. Binary Code: The Language of Computers

Computers don't understand human language. Instead, they rely on a system called **binary**, which is a base-2 numeral system. This system uses only two digits: **0** and **1**. Each **bit** (short for "binary

19

digit") can either be a 0 or a 1. These bits are the building blocks of all computer operations.

Real-world example: When you send a message to a friend via text, your phone converts each letter of your message into a sequence of bits. For example, the letter "A" might be represented as **01000001** in binary code. This binary code is then processed and displayed on your screen.

2. The Role of Processors

The **processor** (also known as the **central processing unit**, or **CPU**) is the brain of the computer. It executes instructions from programs by processing binary data. The CPU takes in instructions written in programming languages (which are human-readable), converts them into machine code (binary), and then performs the necessary calculations or actions.

Real-world example: Suppose you open a word processor to type a document. When you press a key, the keyboard sends a signal to the CPU. The CPU converts the key press into a binary signal, interprets it as the letter you pressed, and displays it on the screen. All of this happens almost instantaneously.

3. Storage: Storing and Retrieving Data

Classical computers also rely on storage devices like **hard drives** and **solid-state drives (SSDs)** to save data for later use. These devices store large amounts of binary data, which the CPU retrieves and processes when needed.

Real-world example: When you save a document on your computer, it's converted into a series of 0s and 1s and stored on your hard drive. Later, when you want to access the document, the computer retrieves these bits and reconstructs the document for you to view.

The Limitations of Classical Computing:

While classical computing is incredibly powerful and forms the foundation of modern technology, it does have its limitations, especially when it comes to handling certain types of complex problems. Let's explore some of these limitations:

1. Processing Power and Speed

Classical computers rely on the processing power of the CPU to handle instructions one at a time. While CPUs can execute billions of instructions per second, they are still fundamentally constrained by their architecture. The more complex a task becomes, the more time it takes to process.

Real-world example: Imagine trying to find the fastest route between multiple locations on a map. Classical computers are great at solving smaller problems, but when the number of locations increases, the number of calculations needed increases exponentially, making it difficult to solve large, complex problems quickly.

2. Memory Limitations

The storage capacity of classical computers is finite, meaning there's a limit to how much data they can hold and process at once. As the demand for computing power grows, classical computers require more memory and processing units to keep up.

Real-world example: Running multiple programs on your computer at once—like a web browser, email client, and music player—can cause it to slow down. This happens because the computer has to manage all the programs using its limited memory resources, and too many tasks can overwhelm the system.

3. Sequential Processing

Classical computers solve problems sequentially, meaning they tackle one calculation or task at a time. While this is effective for many everyday tasks, it becomes inefficient for problems that require simultaneous calculations, especially when the number of possible combinations or variables increases.

Real-world example: In optimization problems (like scheduling a series of flights to minimize delays), classical computers might need to go through each possible solution one by one. As the number of variables increases, the time it takes to find the best solution grows exponentially, making it impractical for very large-scale problems.

Why Quantum Computing is Needed:

Classical computers have served us well in the past and continue to perform many tasks effectively. However, they are limited in their ability to solve certain complex problems, especially those requiring massive amounts of data to be processed or needing simultaneous exploration of many possibilities.

Here's where **quantum computing** comes in. Quantum computers leverage quantum mechanical principles, such as **superposition** and **entanglement**, to perform many calculations at once, rather than sequentially. This ability to process many possibilities simultaneously allows quantum computers to solve problems much faster than classical computers, especially when dealing with tasks that involve massive datasets or complex calculations.

For example, quantum computing can potentially revolutionize **cryptography** by breaking existing encryption methods, or **drug discovery** by simulating molecular structures more efficiently than classical computers.

Key Differences Between Classical and Quantum Computing:

Feature	Classical Computing	Quantum Computing
Basic Unit	Bit (0 or 1)	Qubit (0, 1, or both at the same time due to superposition)
Processing	Sequential: One calculation at a time	Parallel: Multiple calculations simultaneously
Processing Power	Limited by Moore's Law and clock speed	Exponentially faster for certain types of problems
Problem-Solving Approach	Step-by-step calculations	Quantum superposition allows for parallel problem-solving
Memory	Finite and requires optimization	Can represent vast amounts of data using qubits and entanglement

Conclusion:

Classical computing has shaped the modern world and continues to serve as the backbone of most of our digital devices. However, as the complexity of problems continues to increase, classical computing is starting to hit its limits. Quantum computing promises to push beyond these constraints by leveraging the unique properties of quantum mechanics to solve problems in ways classical computers cannot.

In the next chapter, we will dive deeper into the principles of quantum mechanics, which form the foundation of quantum computing. By understanding how quantum systems behave, we can better appreciate why quantum computers hold such potential for the future.

CHAPTER 3

THE PRINCIPLES OF QUANTUM MECHANICS

Quantum mechanics is the fundamental theory that describes how particles behave at the microscopic level — smaller than atoms. It defies the classical laws of physics that govern our everyday world and introduces concepts that can seem strange, yet are essential for understanding quantum computing. In this chapter, we will explore some key principles of quantum mechanics, including **wave-particle duality**, **superposition**, **entanglement**, and **quantum interference**.

Real-World Example: Wave-Particle Duality Using Light

One of the first steps to understanding quantum mechanics is grasping the concept of **wave-particle duality**. This principle states that, at the quantum level, particles like light can behave as both **waves** and **particles** depending on how they are observed. This is a departure from classical physics, where light was traditionally thought of as either a particle or a wave, but never both.

Wave Behavior of Light:

Light can be thought of as a **wave** because it exhibits characteristics like interference and diffraction. For example, when light passes through two slits, it can create an interference pattern, similar to the ripples formed when two stones are thrown into a pond. These ripples overlap and create areas of constructive and destructive interference. This wave-like behavior of light was demonstrated in the famous **double-slit experiment**, where light shining through two slits creates an interference pattern on the other side, much like water waves.

Particle Behavior of Light:

On the other hand, light can also act as a **particle**, known as a **photon**. This was demonstrated by **Max Planck** and **Albert Einstein**, who showed that light can be absorbed or emitted in discrete packets, or quanta, called photons. In phenomena like the **photoelectric effect**, light striking a metal surface can cause electrons to be ejected, but only if the light has a certain energy level. This can only be explained by considering light as made up of particles (photons) rather than waves.

The Double-Slit Experiment:

The **double-slit experiment** is a classic demonstration of wave-particle duality. When light (or even electrons) is passed through two slits and observed, it creates an interference pattern on a screen, similar to how waves behave. However, when individual photons (particles of light) are fired through one at a time, they still form an interference pattern, as if each photon is interfering with itself, acting like a wave.

Here's the truly strange part: If we try to observe which slit the photon passes through, the interference pattern disappears, and the photon behaves like a particle again. This suggests that the very act of observing the particle alters its behavior. This phenomenon is known as **wave function collapse**.

This idea is foundational for quantum mechanics — particles do not have definite properties until they are measured. This principle leads us into the heart of quantum mechanics: **superposition**, **entanglement**, and **quantum interference**.

Key Quantum Concepts:

1. Superposition: Being in Multiple States at Once

In the classical world, an object is either one thing or another. A coin is either heads or tails, a light bulb is either on or off. However, in the quantum world, particles can exist in **multiple states at once**. This is known as **superposition**. For example, a quantum particle (like a qubit in a quantum computer) can be in both the "0" state and the "1" state simultaneously.

Real-World Example: Think of a spinning coin. While it's spinning, it is neither heads nor tails, but in a state that combines both. The coin only "decides" whether it's heads or tails when you stop it and measure the outcome. This is similar to how quantum particles can exist in multiple states until they are observed.

In quantum computing, **superposition** is a key reason why quantum computers can perform certain calculations much faster than classical computers. While classical bits can only be either 0 or 1, quantum bits (qubits) can be in a superposition of both 0 and 1 at the same time, allowing quantum computers to process many possibilities simultaneously.

2. Entanglement: Instantaneous Connection Across Distances

Entanglement is another central concept in quantum mechanics. When two quantum particles (such as photons or electrons) become entangled, their properties become linked, meaning the state of one particle will instantly affect the state of the other, no matter how far apart they are. This happens even if the particles are separated by vast distances, seemingly defying the speed of light.

Real-World Example: Imagine you have two entangled dice. If you roll one die, you immediately know what number the other die will show, even if it's on the other side of the world. This "spooky action at a distance," as Einstein called it, is one of the most puzzling and intriguing aspects of quantum mechanics.

In quantum computing, entanglement is used to link qubits in a quantum computer, allowing them to work together in ways that classical bits cannot, leading to exponential speed-ups in certain types of calculations.

3. Quantum Interference: Enhancing and Canceling Out Possibilities

Quantum interference occurs when the probabilities associated with different quantum states combine, either enhancing or canceling each other out. Just like the interference patterns created by waves, quantum particles can interfere with each other, producing patterns that reflect the likelihood of certain outcomes.

Real-World Example: Think about dropping two pebbles into a pond. The ripples from each pebble will spread out and overlap, creating areas where the waves combine and grow bigger (constructive interference) and areas where the waves cancel each other out (destructive interference). In the quantum world, particles (like photons or electrons) exhibit similar behaviors, and their likelihood of landing in a particular state can interfere with each other.

In quantum computing, interference is a powerful tool. By carefully controlling how qubits interfere, quantum computers can amplify the probabilities of the correct answers and cancel out incorrect ones, which makes quantum algorithms much faster for certain types of problems.

Summary of Key Principles:

Principle	Description	Real-World Example
Wave-Particle Duality	Particles like light exhibit both wave-like and particle-like behavior.	Light can form interference patterns, but also be absorbed as photons.
Superposition	Particles can exist in multiple states at once until measured.	A quantum bit (qubit) can be both 0 and 1 simultaneously.
Entanglement	Two particles become linked, affecting each other instantly, regardless of distance.	Entangled dice: Roll one and know the result of the other instantly.
Quantum Interference	Probabilities of quantum states combine, amplifying or canceling each other out.	Interference patterns created by light passing through slits.

Conclusion:

In this chapter, we've introduced some of the fundamental principles of quantum mechanics — wave-particle duality, superposition, entanglement, and quantum interference. These principles challenge our classical understanding of the world and are the foundation upon which quantum computing is built.

As we continue, we will see how these quantum behaviors are harnessed in quantum computers to solve problems that are practically impossible for classical computers. Understanding these concepts is crucial for appreciating the potential of quantum computing and its future impact on various fields. In the next chapter, we will dive deeper into **qubits**, the quantum equivalent of classical bits, and how they form the building blocks of quantum computers.

CHAPTER 4

QUBITS – THE BUILDING BLOCKS OF QUANTUM COMPUTERS

In the world of classical computing, the basic unit of information is the **bit**. A bit can only be in one of two states at any given time: **0** or **1**. However, quantum computing operates on a different level, using a fundamentally different kind of data unit known as the **qubit** (quantum bit). In this chapter, we'll explore the unique properties of qubits and how they allow quantum computers to perform calculations far beyond the capabilities of classical systems.

What is a Qubit?

A **qubit** is the quantum counterpart to a classical bit. Just like a bit, a qubit can represent information, but with a significant difference: **a qubit can exist in multiple states at once**. This property arises from the fundamental principles of **quantum mechanics**, particularly **superposition**.

A classical bit can only be in one of two states:

33

- **0**
- **1**

In contrast, a qubit can exist in a **superposition** of both **0 and 1** at the same time. This ability to hold multiple possibilities is what allows quantum computers to process information in parallel, significantly enhancing their computational power.

Real-World Example: Flipping a Coin

To better understand **superposition**, let's use a real-world analogy: **flipping a coin**.

- When you flip a coin, while it's in the air, it's not strictly in a state of heads or tails. Instead, it's in a **superposition** of both heads and tails at the same time. It is only when you catch the coin or let it land that you observe it and it "decides" whether it is heads or tails.

This is similar to how a qubit behaves. While the qubit is in superposition, it holds a combination of both the 0 and 1 states simultaneously. However, once the qubit is measured (just like observing the coin when it lands), it "collapses" into either state 0 or 1.

The power of quantum computing comes from the fact that a qubit can represent multiple possibilities at once, allowing quantum computers to explore many solutions simultaneously, rather than one after another like classical computers.

How Qubits Represent Data

While classical bits represent information in binary (either 0 or 1), qubits leverage the principles of quantum mechanics to represent data in a far more complex way:

1. **Superposition**: As mentioned earlier, a qubit can exist in a superposition of both 0 and 1 simultaneously. This allows quantum computers to handle a vast amount of information at once. For example, two qubits can exist in a superposition of four states: 00, 01, 10, and 11. As the number of qubits increases, the number of possible states grows exponentially. This ability to represent many combinations at once is what gives quantum computers their remarkable potential for parallel computation.

2. **Entanglement**: Another key feature of qubits is **entanglement**, which allows qubits to become linked together in such a way that the state of one qubit can instantaneously affect the state of another, regardless of the distance between them. This "spooky action at a distance" enables quantum computers to process and manipulate information in a highly interconnected way,

facilitating complex calculations that classical systems can't handle efficiently.

3. **Quantum Interference**: Quantum interference allows quantum computers to amplify the probability of correct answers and cancel out wrong ones. By carefully controlling the interference of qubits, quantum computers can improve the likelihood of reaching the right solution.

Qubits in Action: Classical vs Quantum Computers

To better understand the power of qubits, let's compare them to classical bits in action. A classical computer, using classical bits, would solve a problem by processing one possibility at a time. Imagine you are trying to solve a maze, and the computer tests each path one after another until it finds the correct solution.

A quantum computer, on the other hand, using qubits in superposition, can test all possible paths at once. It can evaluate many potential solutions simultaneously, vastly speeding up the process. Once the solution is found, the qubits "collapse" to a single state (just like the coin landing on heads or tails) and reveal the answer.

Real-World Example: Quantum Speedup with Qubits

Let's take a real-world problem to understand this difference in computational power. Imagine you're trying to search for a specific number in an unsorted list of 1 million numbers.

- **Classical Search**: A classical computer would check each number one by one until it finds the correct one, taking approximately 1 million checks.
- **Quantum Search (Grover's Algorithm)**: A quantum computer can use a quantum algorithm like **Grover's algorithm** to find the number in approximately the square root of the number of checks (about 1,000 checks). This is a massive speedup, and it shows how qubits in superposition can handle far more information than classical bits.

The Importance of Qubits in Quantum Computing

Qubits are crucial because they allow quantum computers to process exponentially more data compared to classical computers. When quantum computers scale to large numbers of qubits, they will be able to solve problems that were previously deemed impossible due to the sheer complexity or size of the task.

For example:

37

- **Cryptography**: With the ability to represent multiple possibilities at once, quantum computers can break existing encryption systems by factoring large numbers much faster than classical computers.

- **Optimization**: Quantum computers can tackle optimization problems (such as finding the best route for a delivery truck) far more efficiently by simultaneously considering all possible routes.

- **Drug Discovery**: Quantum computers could simulate molecules and chemical reactions with incredible accuracy, accelerating the development of new medicines.

Visualizing Qubits: A Simple Example

Imagine you have a pair of qubits. Each qubit can be in one of four states:

1. **00**
2. **01**
3. **10**
4. **11**

But, due to superposition, these qubits can exist in a state where they represent **all four states simultaneously**. This means that a quantum computer with two qubits can process four possibilities at once.

Now, imagine adding a third qubit:

- A system of three qubits can represent **eight states simultaneously** (000, 001, 010, 011, 100, 101, 110, 111).

As the number of qubits increases, the number of possible states grows exponentially. For N qubits, a quantum computer can represent **2^N** different states at once. This exponential scaling is what makes quantum computing so powerful.

Conclusion:

Qubits are the heart of quantum computing, allowing it to break free from the limitations of classical computing. By leveraging superposition, entanglement, and interference, quantum computers can process massive amounts of information in parallel, enabling them to solve complex problems that would take classical computers millennia to solve. In the next chapter, we'll dive into how quantum gates manipulate qubits to perform calculations, bringing us even closer to understanding the full potential of quantum computing.

CHAPTER 5

SUPERPOSITION – MORE THAN JUST A 1 OR 0

One of the most fundamental principles of quantum mechanics that distinguishes it from classical physics is **superposition**. At its core, superposition allows quantum particles to exist in multiple states at once. This phenomenon is not just a theoretical curiosity—it has profound implications for quantum computing and is one of the main reasons why quantum computers can process vast amounts of data much faster than classical computers. In this chapter, we will explain the concept of superposition, provide a real-world example, and explore why it is so crucial in the context of quantum computing.

What is Superposition?

In classical computing, a **bit** can be in only one of two possible states at any given time: **0** or **1**. This binary system forms the basis of how classical computers process and store data. However, quantum computing is fundamentally different. A **qubit** (the quantum counterpart of a bit) can be in a state that is a **superposition** of both 0 and 1 simultaneously.

Superposition means that a quantum system, such as a qubit, doesn't have a definite state (0 or 1) until it is measured. Instead, it exists in a blend of both possibilities, and only when we observe it does it "collapse" into one of the two states.

Think of it like a **spinning coin**: while it's spinning, it's not just heads or tails—it's a mix of both. Only when the coin lands do we observe whether it's heads or tails. Similarly, qubits in superposition exist in a probabilistic mix of both 0 and 1 until we measure them.

Real-World Example: Schrödinger's Cat

One of the most famous thought experiments to illustrate superposition is **Schrödinger's cat**. Proposed by physicist **Erwin Schrödinger** in 1935, this thought experiment involves a cat inside a sealed box with a radioactive atom and a vial of poison. If the atom decays, the poison is released and the cat dies; if the atom does not decay, the cat survives.

Now, according to quantum mechanics, the radioactive atom can be in a superposition of decayed and non-decayed states until we observe it. In this scenario, until the box is opened, the cat is in a superposition of being both dead and alive at the same time. It's only when the box is opened (i.e., when we measure it) that the cat "collapses" into one of the two definite states—alive or dead.

This paradox highlights the strange and non-intuitive nature of quantum mechanics. Just as the atom is in a superposition of both decayed and non-decayed states, the cat is in a superposition of both alive and dead states, existing simultaneously in both possibilities until we observe it.

Note: Schrödinger's cat thought experiment is a way of illustrating the weirdness of quantum mechanics—it's not meant to be taken literally, but it helps us understand the concept of superposition at a macroscopic scale.

How Superposition Works in Quantum Computing

In quantum computing, superposition allows qubits to represent both 0 and 1 at the same time. This ability enables quantum computers to perform many calculations in parallel, which vastly increases their computational power compared to classical computers.

For example:

- A single classical bit can be in only one state at a time—either 0 or 1.
- A single qubit in superposition, however, can be in a state that is a combination of 0 and 1, meaning it holds both values at once.

42

Imagine you are trying to solve a problem with four possible outcomes. A classical computer would check each outcome one by one, while a quantum computer could evaluate all four possible outcomes simultaneously, thanks to superposition.

The Power of Superposition in Action

The true power of superposition comes when quantum computers scale up. With just a few qubits, quantum computers can process an exponentially larger number of possibilities than classical computers.

For example:

- **1 classical bit**: 2 possible states (0 or 1).
- **2 classical bits**: 4 possible states (00, 01, 10, 11).
- **3 classical bits**: 8 possible states (000, 001, 010, 011, 100, 101, 110, 111).

Now, consider **3 qubits** in superposition:

- A quantum computer can represent **all 8 possible states simultaneously**, thanks to superposition. In other words, it doesn't have to check each state one by one like a classical computer. Instead, it can explore all possibilities at once.

As you add more qubits, the number of possible states grows exponentially. For N qubits, a quantum computer can represent 2^N states at the same time. This is where quantum computers have the potential to massively outperform classical computers on certain tasks.

Real-World Example: Quantum Speedup Using Superposition

Let's take the example of searching for a specific item in an unsorted database. With classical computers, you would need to check each entry one by one. If the database has 1 million items, the classical computer would need to check up to 1 million entries before finding the correct one.

A quantum computer, on the other hand, can take advantage of superposition. Using **Grover's algorithm**, a quantum computer can search an unsorted database in approximately the **square root of the total number of items**. For 1 million items, a quantum computer can find the correct answer in about 1,000 steps, offering a significant speedup compared to classical search methods.

The Role of Superposition in Quantum Algorithms

Superposition is a key feature in many quantum algorithms that provide speedups over classical algorithms. For example:

- **Shor's algorithm** (for factoring large numbers) leverages superposition to break down the task into many parallel computations.
- **Grover's algorithm** (for searching databases) uses superposition to examine multiple possibilities simultaneously, speeding up the search process.

In both cases, superposition allows the quantum computer to process multiple potential solutions at once, reducing the time it takes to solve complex problems.

The Limitations of Superposition

While superposition provides quantum computers with their incredible potential, it is not without challenges:

- **Decoherence**: Superposition is fragile. External interference, such as vibrations or temperature changes, can cause the qubits to lose their superposition and collapse into a single state prematurely.
- **Measurement**: Once a qubit in superposition is measured, it "collapses" to a single state (either 0 or 1),

losing its superposition. This is one reason why quantum computing algorithms need to be carefully designed to leverage superposition before measurement.

Conclusion:

Superposition is one of the most powerful features of quantum computing. It allows qubits to hold multiple possibilities at once, enabling quantum computers to solve problems far faster than classical computers. By exploiting this principle, quantum computers can process vast amounts of data simultaneously, making them well-suited for tasks like cryptography, optimization, and drug discovery.

In the next chapter, we will explore **entanglement**, another key quantum concept, which allows qubits to be linked together in ways that classical bits cannot, further enhancing the power of quantum computing. Understanding superposition is crucial for appreciating the unique abilities of quantum computers, and it lays the foundation for understanding how quantum systems work together to solve complex problems.

CHAPTER 6

ENTANGLEMENT – SPOOKY ACTION AT A DISTANCE

One of the most fascinating and perplexing aspects of quantum mechanics is **entanglement**. It is a phenomenon so strange that Albert Einstein famously referred to it as "**spooky action at a distance**." This chapter will explain what entanglement is, why it baffled even the greatest minds in physics, and how it plays a crucial role in quantum computing and communication.

What is Entanglement?

Quantum entanglement is a phenomenon in which two or more quantum particles become linked together in such a way that the state of one particle cannot be described independently of the state of the others, no matter how far apart they are. In other words, the behavior of one entangled particle is directly tied to the behavior of another, even if they are separated by vast distances.

When two particles are entangled, they share a **quantum state**. If you measure one particle, you immediately know the state of the other, regardless of how far apart they are. This instantaneous connection happens faster than the speed of light, which is what led Einstein to call it "spooky action." Entanglement seems to violate the principles of classical physics, where information cannot travel faster than the speed of light.

Real-World Example: Einstein's Quote on Entanglement

In 1935, Albert Einstein, along with his colleagues Boris Podolsky and Nathan Rosen, published a paper that questioned the completeness of quantum mechanics. They proposed what became known as the **EPR paradox (Einstein-Podolsky-Rosen paradox)**. The paradox described a situation where two particles, once entangled, would remain linked, even if they were separated by large distances.

Einstein famously referred to this kind of connection as **"spooky action at a distance."** He was skeptical of quantum mechanics because it implied that information about one particle could instantaneously affect the state of another particle, no matter how far apart they were. This seemed to contradict the principle of **locality**, which states that objects are only directly influenced by their immediate surroundings.

However, Einstein's skepticism did not stop quantum mechanics from advancing. The EPR paradox led to further investigations, most notably **Bell's Theorem**.

Bell's Theorem and Experiment:

In 1964, physicist **John Bell** proposed a mathematical theorem (known as **Bell's Theorem**) that showed that **if quantum mechanics were correct**, then entanglement would lead to correlations between particles that could not be explained by any theory based on local hidden variables (classical physics). In simpler terms, Bell's Theorem demonstrated that quantum entanglement predicts that particles can influence each other in ways that classical physics cannot explain.

To test this, physicists needed an experiment to measure the **correlations** between entangled particles. In the 1970s, experiments led by physicists **Alain Aspect** and others confirmed that the correlations predicted by quantum mechanics were real. This provided strong evidence in favor of quantum mechanics and entanglement, confirming that the "spooky action" Einstein had criticized was not only real, but fundamental to the quantum world.

How Does Entanglement Work?

Let's break it down with a simple analogy to understand entanglement better:

Imagine you have two entangled dice. You roll one die, and the result is **immediately known** on the other die, no matter how far apart they are. If you roll a **6** on one die, you will instantly know the other die will also show a **6**, even if it is on the other side of the planet.

This is similar to how entangled particles behave. If two electrons are entangled, for example, measuring the spin of one electron (whether it's spinning "up" or "down") will immediately reveal the spin of the other, even if the electrons are light-years apart.

Key Features of Entanglement:

1. **Instantaneous Correlation**: When one entangled particle is measured, the other particle's state is determined instantaneously, regardless of the distance between them.

2. **No Signal Transmission**: Entanglement does not involve the transmission of information between particles faster than light. The particles are simply in a shared state, so once one is measured, the other's state is "known."

3. **Non-locality**: This instantaneous influence between entangled particles happens **instantaneously**, which violates classical ideas of locality (the idea that objects are only influenced by their immediate surroundings).

Applications of Entanglement in Quantum Communication

Entanglement isn't just a theoretical curiosity—it has real-world applications that are making quantum technology possible today. Two key areas where entanglement is applied are **quantum communication** and **quantum computing**.

1. Quantum Cryptography (Quantum Key Distribution)

One of the most promising applications of quantum entanglement is in **quantum cryptography**, particularly in a process called **Quantum Key Distribution (QKD)**. QKD uses the principles of quantum mechanics to create unbreakable encryption.

In quantum cryptography, entangled particles are used to generate a shared secret key between two parties. If an eavesdropper tries to intercept the quantum communication, the act of measuring the entangled particles will disturb their state and reveal the presence of the intruder. This ensures that the key exchange is secure, as any interference will be immediately detectable.

Real-World Example: **Quantum Internet** – Companies like **China's Quantum Satellite** have already demonstrated successful quantum communication over long distances using entanglement. The quantum internet promises to provide **secure, unhackable communication**, thanks to the fundamental properties of entanglement.

2. Quantum Teleportation

Quantum teleportation is another futuristic application of entanglement. It doesn't involve physically transporting matter from one place to another, but rather transferring the **quantum state** of a particle from one location to another using entanglement.

In this process, two particles become entangled, and the quantum state of one particle is "teleported" to the other particle, without moving the particle itself. This technology could be used for ultra-fast data transfer and secure communication.

Real-World Example: In 2017, **Chinese scientists** successfully demonstrated quantum teleportation by transferring quantum information between two entangled particles over **1,200 kilometers**—the longest distance for quantum teleportation to date.

Entanglement in Quantum Computing

Entanglement plays a crucial role in **quantum computing**, particularly when it comes to **quantum parallelism** and **quantum algorithms**. When qubits are entangled, they can perform multiple computations at once, greatly enhancing the speed and power of quantum computers.

For example, **Shor's algorithm**, which is used to factor large numbers, relies on entangled qubits to explore many possible solutions simultaneously. Entanglement allows quantum computers to exploit the full computational power of qubits, exponentially speeding up certain types of calculations.

Real-World Example: In 2019, **Google's quantum computer** achieved **quantum supremacy** by solving a specific problem faster than the most powerful classical computer could, in part due to the use of entangled qubits in its quantum algorithm.

Conclusion:

Entanglement is one of the most mind-bending concepts in quantum mechanics, and it is central to the potential of quantum technologies. Despite its mysterious nature, entanglement has proven to be real through groundbreaking experiments like Bell's Theorem and Alain Aspect's work. Today, it is being used in practical applications like quantum cryptography and quantum computing, and its impact on communication and information technology is only just beginning to unfold.

As we move forward, quantum entanglement will continue to be a cornerstone of the quantum revolution, enabling breakthroughs in computing, communication, and beyond. In the next chapter, we will explore **quantum gates**, how they manipulate qubits, and how quantum computers perform calculations using these fundamental operations.

CHAPTER 7

QUANTUM INTERFERENCE – USING PROBABILITY TO YOUR ADVANTAGE

One of the most powerful features of quantum mechanics is **quantum interference**. This phenomenon allows quantum systems to combine probabilities in such a way that the likelihood of a particular outcome is enhanced, while other possibilities are canceled out. This principle is key to how quantum computers can solve certain problems exponentially faster than classical computers. In this chapter, we'll explore quantum interference, using a real-world analogy to explain the concept, and demonstrate how it plays a crucial role in optimizing quantum calculations.

What is Quantum Interference?

Quantum interference arises from the **wave-like behavior** of particles at the quantum level. According to quantum mechanics, particles such as electrons, photons, or qubits do not have a definite position or state until they are measured. Instead, their positions or states are described by **wave functions**, which represent the probabilities of where the particle might be or what state it might be in.

Interference occurs when two or more waves (or wave functions) combine. Depending on how these waves interact with each other, they can either **amplify** each other (constructive interference) or **cancel each other out** (destructive interference). This behavior is similar to the interference of sound or light waves.

Real-World Example: The Double-Slit Experiment

One of the most famous demonstrations of quantum interference is the **double-slit experiment**, first performed by **Thomas Young** in the early 19th century. Though originally used to demonstrate the wave nature of light, it later became fundamental in understanding quantum mechanics.

The Classical Double-Slit Experiment:

In the classical version of this experiment, a beam of light (or particles like electrons) is directed at a screen with two slits. On the other side of the screen, a detection device (like a photographic plate) captures the light that passes through the slits.

- If light behaves as particles, we would expect to see two bands of light corresponding to the slits, much like if you threw two pebbles in water and observed two sets of waves.

- However, when light behaves as a wave, it passes through both slits at once and the waves interfere with each other. This results in a pattern of alternating light and dark bands, known as an **interference pattern**. The dark bands occur where the waves cancel out (destructive interference), and the light bands occur where the waves reinforce each other (constructive interference).

The Quantum Double-Slit Experiment:

Now, let's apply the same setup to quantum particles, like photons or electrons. When a single particle is fired at the slits one at a time, classical physics would predict it should pass through one slit or the other, resulting in two distinct bands on the detection screen. But what actually happens is far stranger:

- Even though each particle is sent through the slits one by one, it still creates an interference pattern on the screen, just as if it were a wave passing through both slits simultaneously.
- This indicates that the particle exists in a **superposition** of both paths at once, and only when measured does it collapse into a single state (either passing through one slit or the other).

- The interference pattern only emerges when particles are not observed or measured during their travel through the slits. If the experiment is set up to detect which slit the particle passes through, the interference pattern disappears, and the particles behave like classical particles, creating two bands instead of an interference pattern.

This experiment beautifully demonstrates quantum interference, where the probability of the particle's path is influenced by the wave-like nature of its wave function. The quantum state exists in a superposition, with probabilities spreading out, and the interference of these probabilities results in the observed interference pattern.

Quantum Interference in Quantum Computing

Quantum interference plays a critical role in quantum computing, particularly in **quantum algorithms** that rely on the parallelism enabled by superposition. Quantum computers can use interference to manipulate the probabilities of different solutions to an optimization problem, enhancing the probability of finding the correct solution and reducing the likelihood of incorrect solutions.

In classical computers, calculations are performed step by step, and they rely on the deterministic behavior of bits (either 0 or 1). In quantum computers, qubits can exist in a superposition of states, allowing them to explore multiple possibilities at once. Interference is then used to amplify the probability of the correct solutions and cancel out the wrong ones.

Real-World Example: Grover's Algorithm

One of the most well-known quantum algorithms that uses interference is **Grover's algorithm**, which is designed for searching unsorted databases. If you wanted to find a specific item in a database of 1 million entries using a classical computer, you would need to check each item one by one, taking up to 1 million steps.

Quantum computers, however, can search the entire database simultaneously using superposition. Grover's algorithm then uses quantum interference to amplify the probability of finding the correct entry. Over several iterations, the correct answer's probability grows, while the incorrect ones are progressively diminished. In just about $\sqrt{N}$ steps (where N is the number of entries), Grover's algorithm can find the correct item, representing a **quadratic speedup** compared to classical searching methods.

Quantum Parallelism and Interference in Action

To further understand how quantum interference works, consider a simple example of a quantum computer solving an optimization problem. The problem involves finding the best solution from a large set of possibilities. Classical computers would need to evaluate each possibility one by one, while a quantum computer can evaluate many possibilities in parallel using superposition.

After evaluating all the possibilities, the quantum computer uses interference to enhance the probabilities of the best solutions and suppress those that are less likely to be correct. This process is like tuning a guitar: quantum interference adjusts the frequencies (probabilities) of each possible solution, making the correct answer louder (more probable) and the incorrect answers quieter (less probable).

The Significance of Quantum Interference

The ability to manipulate interference in quantum computers is crucial for solving problems that are intractable for classical computers. Quantum interference allows quantum computers to:

- **Enhance the probability of correct outcomes**: By amplifying the correct answers and canceling out the wrong ones, quantum interference can optimize solutions for complex problems.

- **Improve computational efficiency**: Quantum algorithms that use interference, like Grover's algorithm, can provide significant speedups over classical algorithms for tasks like database searching, optimization, and factorization.

- **Solve problems with a large number of variables**: Quantum interference makes it possible to consider and evaluate a vast number of possibilities simultaneously, which is especially useful for solving problems with high-dimensional or complex search spaces, such as machine learning and cryptography.

Conclusion:

Quantum interference is a powerful tool that allows quantum computers to efficiently solve problems by leveraging the wave-like nature of quantum particles. By carefully controlling the interference of qubits, quantum algorithms can explore multiple possibilities at once, amplify the chances of finding the correct solution, and suppress incorrect ones. This ability to optimize calculations is what gives quantum computers their incredible potential.

As we continue to explore quantum algorithms, we'll see how interference is used in various algorithms to accelerate problem-solving and optimize solutions. In the next chapter, we will look at how **quantum gates** work, manipulating qubits and their states to perform calculations and operations essential to quantum computing.

CHAPTER 8

QUANTUM GATES AND CIRCUITS

Just as classical computers rely on **logic gates** (such as AND, OR, NOT) to perform calculations, quantum computers also rely on **quantum gates** to manipulate qubits and perform computations. However, unlike classical gates, which process bits in a deterministic way, quantum gates work in a probabilistic manner, leveraging the unique properties of quantum mechanics like **superposition** and **entanglement**. In this chapter, we will explore how quantum gates work, how they differ from classical gates, and their role in building quantum circuits.

Classical Logic Gates: A Quick Overview

To understand how quantum gates function, let's first review how logic gates operate in classical computing.

In classical computing, **logic gates** are fundamental building blocks that perform logical operations on **bits** (binary digits). These gates take in binary inputs (0 or 1) and produce a binary output (0 or 1). Here are a few common classical gates:

1. **AND Gate**: This gate outputs **1** only when both inputs are **1**. Otherwise, the output is **0**.
   - Example: Input (1, 1) → Output: 1
   - Input (1, 0) → Output: 0
   - Input (0, 0) → Output: 0
2. **OR Gate**: This gate outputs **1** when at least one of the inputs is **1**.
   - Example: Input (1, 0) → Output: 1
   - Input (0, 0) → Output: 0
   - Input (1, 1) → Output: 1
3. **NOT Gate**: This gate flips the input; if the input is **0**, the output is **1**, and if the input is **1**, the output is **0**.
   - Example: Input (1) → Output: 0
   - Input (0) → Output: 1

These classical logic gates form the basis for performing all logical operations in a classical computer. However, quantum computers use quantum gates, which manipulate **qubits** in a much more sophisticated way.

Quantum Gates: Manipulating Qubits

Quantum gates manipulate qubits, the fundamental units of quantum computing. Unlike classical bits, qubits can exist in superposition, meaning they can represent both 0 and 1 simultaneously. Quantum gates are responsible for changing the states of qubits in various ways, based on the principles of quantum mechanics such as **superposition** and **entanglement**.

There are several types of quantum gates, each with its own function. Quantum gates act on one or more qubits and are represented by **unitary matrices** (mathematical operations that preserve the total probability). Let's look at some of the most common quantum gates and how they differ from their classical counterparts.

Common Quantum Gates

1. **Hadamard Gate (H Gate)**: The Hadamard gate is one of the most important quantum gates. It takes a single qubit and places it into **superposition**, meaning it turns a qubit that is in state 0 ($|0\rangle$) or 1 ($|1\rangle$) into a superposition of both states. This gate is the quantum equivalent of a **flip** in classical computing but with a twist: it creates an equal probability of being in both states.

    o   **Operation**: The Hadamard gate transforms a qubit as follows:

        ▪ $H|0\rangle \rightarrow (|0\rangle + |1\rangle) / \sqrt{2}$
        ▪ $H|1\rangle \rightarrow (|0\rangle - |1\rangle) / \sqrt{2}$

    o   **Real-World Example**: If you have a qubit in state $|0\rangle$ (representing 0), applying the Hadamard gate will put the qubit in a state where it is equally likely to be found as 0 or 1 when measured, just like flipping a coin.

2. **Pauli-X Gate (X Gate)**: The Pauli-X gate is a quantum analog of the **NOT gate** in classical computing. It flips the state of a qubit—if the qubit is in state $|0\rangle$, it changes to $|1\rangle$, and vice versa.

   o **Operation**:

      ▪ $X|0\rangle \rightarrow |1\rangle$

      ▪ $X|1\rangle \rightarrow |0\rangle$

   o **Real-World Example**: If a qubit is in state $|0\rangle$ (like a classical bit of 0), applying the Pauli-X gate would flip it to $|1\rangle$, just like flipping a classical bit.

3. **CNOT Gate (Controlled-NOT Gate)**: The CNOT gate is a **two-qubit gate** that flips the state of the second qubit (the target qubit) if the first qubit (the control qubit) is in the state $|1\rangle$. If the control qubit is in state $|0\rangle$, the target qubit remains unchanged.

   o **Operation**:

      ▪ If the control qubit is $|0\rangle$: The target qubit remains unchanged.

      ▪ If the control qubit is $|1\rangle$: The target qubit is flipped.

   o **Real-World Example**: Imagine two entangled qubits. If the control qubit is in state $|0\rangle$, the target qubit stays the same. But if the control qubit is in

66

state $|1\rangle$, the target qubit will flip, demonstrating how qubits can influence each other's states via entanglement.

4. **Phase Shift Gate (S Gate, T Gate)**: The phase shift gate alters the phase of a qubit's state without changing its probability of being measured as 0 or 1. The **S gate** applies a phase of 90 degrees, while the **T gate** applies a phase of 45 degrees.

   o **Operation**:

      ▪ $S|0\rangle = |0\rangle$

      ▪ $S|1\rangle = i|1\rangle$ (where i is the imaginary unit)

   o **Real-World Example**: Phase gates don't change the probabilities of a qubit's state, but they change how the qubit behaves in the context of quantum interference, affecting the outcome when multiple qubits interact.

5. **Toffoli Gate (CCNOT Gate)**: The Toffoli gate is a **three-qubit gate** that acts as a controlled-controlled-NOT operation. It flips the third qubit (target) only if both the first and second qubits (controls) are in state $|1\rangle$.

   o **Real-World Example**: The Toffoli gate can be thought of as a more complex version of the CNOT gate, where two control qubits are required to trigger the flipping of the target qubit.

Building Quantum Circuits

In classical computing, logic gates are combined to build circuits that can perform any computation. The same is true for quantum computing, but instead of bits, quantum circuits manipulate qubits using quantum gates. Quantum circuits are built by connecting different quantum gates in sequence to solve a problem.

- **Quantum Circuit Design**: Just like classical circuits, quantum circuits are composed of multiple gates that perform operations on qubits. These gates are combined in specific sequences to create quantum algorithms. The quantum circuit model allows us to break down complex quantum computations into smaller, manageable steps.

- **Quantum Parallelism**: The power of quantum circuits comes from their ability to operate on multiple qubits in superposition. This allows quantum circuits to explore multiple solutions simultaneously. Interference is then used to filter out the incorrect solutions and amplify the probability of the correct ones.

Real-World Example: Quantum Computing vs Classical Computing in Circuit Design

To better understand the difference between classical and quantum circuits, let's compare them with a simple problem: **searching for a particular number in an unsorted list**.

- **Classical Circuit**: A classical circuit uses **classical bits** and logic gates (AND, OR, NOT) to search through the list, checking one number at a time. The process is sequential, meaning it will take **N steps** to find the correct number in a list of **N items**.

- **Quantum Circuit**: A quantum circuit, using qubits in superposition, can search the entire list simultaneously. Quantum gates manipulate qubits to explore multiple possibilities at once, and interference amplifies the probability of finding the correct answer. This process is much faster, allowing the quantum computer to search through **N** items in about $\sqrt{N}$ steps.

Conclusion

Quantum gates are the fundamental building blocks of quantum circuits, just as classical logic gates are for classical circuits. However, unlike classical gates, quantum gates leverage the unique properties of quantum mechanics—such as superposition, entanglement, and interference—to manipulate qubits in ways that classical computers cannot achieve.

By combining quantum gates in sequences to create quantum circuits, quantum computers can solve complex problems exponentially faster than classical computers. As we continue to explore quantum algorithms, we will see how these quantum circuits enable breakthroughs in fields like cryptography, optimization, and machine learning.

In the next chapter, we will explore **quantum algorithms**, which are the sets of instructions that guide quantum circuits to solve specific problems, demonstrating the practical power of quantum gates and circuits in action.

CHAPTER 9

QUANTUM ALGORITHMS – THE HEART OF QUANTUM COMPUTING

Quantum algorithms are the driving force behind the power of quantum computers. These algorithms leverage the principles of quantum mechanics—such as **superposition, entanglement**, and **interference**—to solve problems more efficiently than classical algorithms. In this chapter, we'll explore quantum algorithms, focusing on how they achieve **quantum speedups**. We'll also compare a classical search algorithm with **Grover's quantum search algorithm**, highlighting the advantages that quantum algorithms offer.

What Are Quantum Algorithms?

Quantum algorithms are a set of instructions designed to solve problems using quantum computers. They harness quantum mechanical properties to process information in ways that classical computers cannot. Quantum algorithms perform computations using **qubits** (quantum bits), which can exist in multiple states simultaneously (thanks to **superposition**), and

71

entanglement allows for the creation of complex interconnections between qubits that enable faster computation.

One of the most important features of quantum algorithms is their ability to **explore multiple solutions at once,** thanks to quantum parallelism. This ability significantly speeds up the process of finding solutions, especially for complex problems that would take classical computers an impractically long time to solve.

Real-World Example: Classical vs Quantum Search Algorithms

Let's explore a **classical search algorithm** and **Grover's quantum search algorithm** to understand the quantum speedup.

Classical Search Algorithm:

In a classical computer, searching through an unsorted database or list of items is a straightforward process. A classical search algorithm, such as **linear search**, looks at one item at a time and checks if it matches the desired search query.

- **Step-by-step process**:
    1. Start at the first item in the list.
    2. Check if it matches the search query.
    3. If it does, stop and return the item.
    4. If not, move to the next item and repeat until the end of the list is reached.

This process is sequential, and in the worst case, it requires checking all **N** items in the list. So, the time complexity for a classical search is **O(N)**, meaning that as the size of the list grows, the time to find the item increases linearly.

Grover's Quantum Search Algorithm:

Grover's algorithm is a quantum search algorithm that solves the same problem—finding a specific item in an unsorted list—but it does so much faster than any classical algorithm. The key difference is that **Grover's algorithm can search the database in $\sqrt{N}$ steps, where N is the number of items in the list. This is a quadratic speedup over the classical approach.

- **How it works**: Grover's algorithm leverages quantum superposition to create a superposition of all possible answers. Then, it applies quantum interference to amplify the probability of the correct answer while diminishing the probabilities of incorrect answers. The algorithm repeats this process several times, gradually increasing the probability of finding the correct answer, until a measurement collapses the superposition to the correct answer.

- **Quantum speedup**: While a classical search algorithm needs to check each element in the list one at a time, Grover's algorithm allows the quantum computer to evaluate all possible solutions in parallel. Thanks to quantum interference, the algorithm focuses on the correct solution, speeding up the search process.

- **Example**: If you're searching through a list of 1 million items, a classical search algorithm might require up to 1 million checks, while Grover's algorithm can find the item in about 1,000 checks, making it **1000 times faster** for this specific example.

Key takeaway: Grover's algorithm is an example of how quantum computers can achieve a significant **speedup** over classical computers for problems that involve searching unsorted data.

Quantum Speedups and Other Quantum Algorithms

While Grover's algorithm is one of the most famous examples, it is just one of many quantum algorithms that offer speedups in various types of problems. Quantum speedup refers to the ability of quantum algorithms to solve problems much faster than classical algorithms by exploiting the unique properties of quantum mechanics. Here's a brief overview of some other quantum algorithms that achieve quantum speedups.

1. Shor's Algorithm (Quantum Factoring):

One of the most groundbreaking quantum algorithms is **Shor's algorithm**, which is designed for factoring large numbers into prime factors. Factoring large numbers is a problem that classical computers struggle with, especially as the size of the numbers increases. Classical algorithms, such as the **general number field sieve**, take an impractical amount of time for very large numbers.

However, Shor's algorithm can factor numbers in **polynomial time**, which is exponentially faster than any known classical algorithm. This quantum speedup has major implications for cryptography, as many encryption systems rely on the difficulty of factoring large numbers (such as RSA encryption).

Real-World Impact: Shor's algorithm could potentially break modern encryption methods, which rely on the fact that factoring large numbers is computationally expensive. Quantum computers could render traditional encryption obsolete, leading to the development of new **quantum-safe cryptography**.

2. Quantum Fourier Transform (QFT):

The **Quantum Fourier Transform** is another quantum algorithm used in problems like **signal processing** and **quantum simulations**. It is the quantum version of the classical **Fast Fourier Transform** (FFT), which decomposes a function into its constituent frequencies.

Quantum computers can perform the Quantum Fourier Transform exponentially faster than classical computers, which is useful in many applications, including solving partial differential equations and performing quantum simulations.

3. Quantum Simulation Algorithms:

Quantum computers are particularly suited for simulating quantum systems, which is a task that classical computers struggle with, especially as the size and complexity of the system increase. Quantum simulation algorithms use quantum mechanics to simulate the behavior of molecules, materials, and chemical reactions.

For example, **quantum chemistry simulations** using quantum computers could revolutionize drug discovery by accurately simulating complex chemical interactions. This is something classical computers cannot do efficiently, especially when dealing with large molecules or interactions between electrons.

Why Quantum Algorithms Matter

Quantum algorithms provide significant speedups for problems that are computationally hard for classical computers. These speedups come from the ability of quantum computers to:

- **Evaluate many possibilities simultaneously** using superposition.
- **Manipulate probabilities** using quantum interference to focus on the most likely solutions.
- **Leverage quantum entanglement** to link qubits and enhance the computational power of quantum systems.

As quantum computers become more powerful, these algorithms will enable breakthroughs in fields such as:

- **Cryptography**: By breaking traditional encryption and leading to the development of new quantum-safe methods.
- **Optimization**: By solving complex optimization problems faster, enabling more efficient solutions in logistics, finance, and manufacturing.
- **Machine Learning**: By speeding up machine learning algorithms and providing better data analysis for large datasets.

Conclusion

Quantum algorithms, like Grover's and Shor's, demonstrate how quantum computing offers a **quantum speedup** over classical computers. These algorithms are key to unlocking the potential of quantum computers, allowing them to solve problems that would take classical computers decades or longer.

As we continue to explore quantum algorithms in future chapters, we will see how these algorithms are applied to real-world problems in cryptography, optimization, and simulation. The development and application of quantum algorithms will be central to the future of quantum computing and its ability to tackle complex challenges across various industries.

CHAPTER 10

SHOR'S ALGORITHM AND THE FUTURE OF CRYPTOGRAPHY

In the world of cryptography, the security of many systems is based on the difficulty of certain mathematical problems, such as factoring large numbers. One of the most widely used encryption methods today, **RSA encryption**, relies on the fact that factoring large numbers is computationally infeasible with classical computers. However, this assumption is being challenged by the advent of quantum computers, particularly with the development of **Shor's algorithm**. In this chapter, we'll introduce Shor's algorithm, explain how it works, and explore its significant implications for modern cryptography.

What is RSA Encryption?

RSA encryption is one of the most widely used public-key encryption schemes. It forms the foundation for securing communications on the internet, such as SSL/TLS for secure browsing, email encryption, and even digital signatures.

The security of RSA encryption relies on the fact that, while it is easy to multiply large prime numbers together, **factoring the**

product of two large primes back into its original prime factors is **extremely difficult**. Here's how it works:

1. **Key Generation**:
   - Two large prime numbers, **p** and **q**, are chosen randomly.
   - Their product, $N = p \times q$, forms part of the public key.
   - The totient function, $\varphi(N)$, is calculated, which is used to determine the encryption and decryption keys.

2. **Encryption**:
   - The sender uses the recipient's public key (which includes **N**) to encrypt the message.

3. **Decryption**:
   - Only the recipient, who knows the private key (derived from **p** and **q**), can decrypt the message by factoring **N** back into **p** and **q**.

The strength of RSA encryption lies in the fact that, given the **public key (N)**, **factoring N** into its prime factors is computationally hard with classical computers, especially when **N** is large (e.g., hundreds of digits).

Real-World Example: How Quantum Computers Can Break RSA Encryption

Quantum computers, particularly through **Shor's algorithm**, can fundamentally change the landscape of cryptography. Shor's algorithm is a quantum algorithm specifically designed for efficiently factoring large numbers, which is precisely the task required to break RSA encryption.

Let's see how Shor's algorithm works and why it's such a game-changer:

Classical Computers and RSA Security:

Classical computers rely on factoring methods like the **general number field sieve** to factor large numbers. For numbers with hundreds of digits (the size used in modern encryption), factoring them using classical algorithms would take **millions of years**. This is why RSA encryption is considered secure with current classical computers.

Shor's Algorithm and Quantum Speedup:

Shor's algorithm takes advantage of quantum mechanics to **factor large numbers exponentially faster** than any classical algorithm. The core idea of Shor's algorithm is based on **quantum parallelism** and the ability to compute certain functions, like

81

periodicity (repeated patterns in numbers), much more efficiently than classical methods.

Here's a simplified breakdown of how Shor's algorithm works:

1. **Quantum Fourier Transform (QFT)** is used to find the period of a function related to the number to be factored.
2. By finding the period, it is possible to efficiently determine factors of a large number, which would be incredibly time-consuming for a classical computer.

In essence, **Shor's algorithm can solve the factoring problem in polynomial time**—a process that would take classical computers exponential time for large numbers.

Implications for Modern Cryptography

The ability of quantum computers to efficiently break RSA encryption poses a significant challenge to modern cryptography. The security of many systems that we rely on today could be compromised once quantum computers reach sufficient size and power. Let's explore the key implications:

1. Breaking RSA and Other Public-Key Cryptosystems

RSA encryption is the backbone of much of the security we use online. If quantum computers can efficiently run Shor's algorithm, they could break the encryption by factoring large numbers in a fraction of the time that classical computers would take. This means that all communications secured with RSA (e.g., emails, online banking transactions) could be decrypted by someone with access to a sufficiently powerful quantum computer.

Beyond RSA, other **public-key cryptosystems**, such as **Diffie-Hellman** (used for secure key exchange) and **Elliptic Curve Cryptography (ECC)**, would also be vulnerable to Shor's algorithm. These systems also rely on the hardness of problems like factoring or the discrete logarithm problem, both of which Shor's algorithm can solve efficiently.

2. Quantum-Safe Cryptography

The threat posed by Shor's algorithm has led to the development of **quantum-safe** or **post-quantum cryptography**. These are cryptographic systems that are resistant to attacks from quantum computers. Researchers are working on algorithms that are difficult for quantum computers to solve, such as those based on **lattice problems**, **hash functions**, and **code-based cryptography**.

Example of Quantum-Safe Cryptography:

- **Lattice-based encryption**: Lattice-based cryptography relies on problems that are computationally hard for both classical and quantum computers, such as the **shortest**

vector problem. These systems are being considered for future encryption standards to replace RSA and ECC.

3. Transition to Post-Quantum Cryptography

As quantum computers develop, there is an ongoing effort to transition from classical cryptographic systems to quantum-safe algorithms. This includes:

- **Quantum Key Distribution (QKD)**: This leverages quantum entanglement and quantum principles to create unbreakable keys for encryption. If a quantum computer tries to eavesdrop on the key exchange, the state of the quantum system would be disturbed, alerting both parties.
- **Hybrid Systems**: For a smooth transition, some experts recommend hybrid cryptosystems that use both classical and quantum-safe algorithms, ensuring secure communication even during the shift to fully quantum-safe encryption methods.

The Race for Quantum Computing and Cryptography

While quantum computers capable of running Shor's algorithm at a large scale are not yet a reality, the possibility is rapidly approaching. The development of **quantum computers** that can break RSA encryption is one of the driving forces behind the push for quantum-safe cryptography. Experts are already preparing for a world where quantum computers can break today's most commonly used cryptosystems, and it's essential to start developing and implementing quantum-resistant encryption methods today.

Conclusion

Shor's algorithm represents one of the most significant challenges to modern cryptography. By efficiently factoring large numbers, quantum computers could render systems like RSA encryption obsolete, posing a risk to the security of many communications and transactions on the internet. However, this challenge has spurred the development of **quantum-safe cryptography**, which aims to create encryption methods that can withstand the power of quantum computing.

As we move forward into the quantum era, it will be essential to adopt new encryption technologies to safeguard our data against quantum threats. The development of quantum computers and quantum-safe encryption will shape the future of secure communication, and understanding Shor's algorithm is a crucial step in preparing for this future.

In the next chapter, we will explore how **quantum cryptography** is already being used to create secure communication channels and how it is expected to evolve with the advancement of quantum technologies.

CHAPTER 11

GROVER'S ALGORITHM – SPEEDING UP SEARCH PROBLEMS

In classical computing, searching through an unsorted database or list is an inherently slow process, especially when the list grows large. The process is often linear, meaning you must examine each item in the list one by one until you find the item you're looking for. For databases containing millions or billions of entries, this becomes incredibly time-consuming. Enter **Grover's algorithm**, a quantum algorithm designed to dramatically speed up the process of searching unsorted databases. In this chapter, we'll explain how Grover's algorithm works, compare it to classical methods, and explore its potential applications in search optimization.

What is Grover's Algorithm?

Grover's algorithm is a quantum algorithm designed to search an unsorted database or solve an unstructured search problem in **quadratic speedup** compared to classical algorithms. It was introduced by **Lov Grover** in 1996 and is one of the most well-known quantum algorithms, particularly because of its ability to dramatically reduce the time required for certain search problems.

The key to Grover's algorithm is its ability to perform **quantum parallelism**, allowing it to search through all possible entries in a database simultaneously. While a classical search algorithm has to check each possibility one by one, Grover's algorithm uses **superposition** and **quantum interference** to evaluate all possibilities at once and find the correct solution in significantly fewer steps.

Real-World Example: Classical Search vs Grover's Algorithm

To understand how Grover's algorithm speeds up the search process, let's compare it to a **classical search algorithm**.

Classical Search Algorithm:

Let's imagine you have an unsorted list of **N** items, and you need to find a specific item. In a classical search algorithm, such as **linear search**, you would:

1. Start at the first item in the list.
2. Check if it matches the target item.
3. If it does, return the item.
4. If it doesn't, move to the next item and repeat the process until the target is found.

In the worst case, you might need to check all **N** items, so the time complexity of a classical search is **O(N)**. If you're searching through a list of **1 million items**, it might take up to 1 million steps to find the correct one.

Grover's Quantum Search Algorithm:

Now, imagine you're using Grover's algorithm to search the same unsorted database. Thanks to **quantum superposition**, Grover's algorithm can evaluate all the entries in the database simultaneously. It does this by placing all potential solutions into a superposition of states and using **quantum interference** to amplify the probability of the correct answer.

Grover's algorithm requires only $\sqrt{N}$ **steps** to find the correct entry, where N is the total number of entries in the list. So, if you have 1 million items in the database, Grover's algorithm can find the target in about **1,000 steps**—a significant speedup compared to the 1 million steps needed for a classical search algorithm.

How Does Grover's Algorithm Work?

Grover's algorithm relies on two key quantum principles: **superposition** and **interference**. Let's break down the steps involved in Grover's algorithm:

89

1. Initialization (Superposition):

Grover's algorithm begins by preparing a superposition of all possible entries in the database. This is done by applying a **Hadamard gate** to the initial qubits, creating a state where each possible solution has an equal probability of being correct.

2. Oracle (Black Box Function):

The next step is to use an **oracle**, a black-box quantum function that marks the solution by flipping the sign of the amplitude of the correct answer. The oracle effectively "identifies" the target item by changing its state, but it does not tell the algorithm where the solution is—only that it has found the correct answer.

3. Amplitude Amplification (Interference):

Grover's algorithm amplifies the probability of the correct solution through a process known as **amplitude amplification**. The algorithm applies a series of quantum operations (including the **Grover diffusion operator**) to increase the probability amplitude of the correct answer while decreasing the probability amplitude of the incorrect answers.

This process works by exploiting **quantum interference**: the amplitude of the correct solution is **constructively interfered**, boosting its probability, while the incorrect solutions are **destructively interfered**, reducing their probabilities.

4. Measurement:

After several iterations of the oracle and amplitude amplification, the probability of measuring the correct solution increases. Eventually, when the quantum state is measured, the algorithm collapses into the state corresponding to the correct solution.

Applications of Grover's Algorithm

Grover's algorithm has significant implications for various fields that require searching through large, unstructured datasets. Here are some potential applications:

1. Search Optimization:

The primary application of Grover's algorithm is in **search optimization**. Any problem that involves searching through large datasets or searching for a solution among many possible candidates can potentially benefit from Grover's algorithm. Examples include:

- Searching through a database of unsorted records (such as searching for a specific user in an unsorted directory).
- Solving combinatorial optimization problems where the goal is to find the best solution from a set of possibilities.

2. Machine Learning:

In machine learning, Grover's algorithm could be used to optimize training and search for optimal parameters in a model. For example, hyperparameter tuning in machine learning models often requires searching through large, unstructured spaces of possible parameter combinations. Grover's algorithm could help accelerate this process by speeding up the search for the best parameters.

3. Cryptanalysis:

Grover's algorithm could also be used in **cryptanalysis**, where it can be used to speed up the process of breaking certain cryptographic schemes. For example, Grover's algorithm can be applied to brute-force attacks on symmetric-key cryptography, reducing the time complexity of trying all possible keys from **$O(2^N)$** to **$O(2^{(N/2)})$**. While this is still computationally hard, it presents a significant advantage for quantum computers over classical systems.

4. Quantum Chemistry:

Grover's algorithm can be used in quantum chemistry to search for specific chemical reactions or molecular configurations. The algorithm's ability to evaluate many configurations simultaneously could help speed up the discovery of new materials, drugs, or chemical processes by finding optimal solutions in large, complex systems.

Quantum Speedup with Grover's Algorithm

Grover's algorithm represents a **quadratic speedup** for unstructured search problems, which is a significant improvement over classical methods. While classical search algorithms take **O(N)** steps, Grover's algorithm can reduce that to **O($\sqrt{N}$)**, providing an exponential advantage as the size of the database grows. This quantum speedup could have far-reaching implications for fields that require fast search capabilities, including:

- **Big Data**: Searching through massive datasets in databases and cloud systems.
- **Optimization Problems**: Solving complex problems like routing, scheduling, and logistics more efficiently.
- **AI and Machine Learning**: Speeding up algorithms that require finding optimal solutions among many possible candidates.

Conclusion

Grover's algorithm is a key quantum algorithm that leverages the unique properties of quantum mechanics to provide an exponential speedup for unstructured search problems. By exploiting **quantum parallelism** and **quantum interference**,

Grover's algorithm can search unsorted databases much faster than classical search algorithms, offering significant advantages in search optimization and other computational tasks.

As quantum computing continues to develop, Grover's algorithm and similar quantum algorithms will become increasingly important tools in a wide range of industries, from cryptography to machine learning and beyond. In the next chapter, we will explore **quantum error correction** and how quantum systems deal with the inherent instability and noise of quantum states, ensuring that quantum computers can reliably perform complex calculations.

CHAPTER 12

QUANTUM SPEEDUP – HOW QUANTUM COMPUTERS CAN SOLVE PROBLEMS FASTER

Quantum computers promise to revolutionize how we solve certain types of problems. Thanks to the unique properties of quantum mechanics—such as **superposition, entanglement,** and **quantum interference**—quantum computers can perform certain calculations much faster than classical computers. This chapter will explore how quantum speedup works, the types of problems quantum computers excel at, and provide real-world examples comparing how long it takes classical and quantum systems to solve problems.

What is Quantum Speedup?

Quantum speedup refers to the ability of quantum computers to solve certain problems exponentially faster than classical computers. Classical computers rely on bits to process information, which can be either **0** or **1**, and they perform calculations one step at a time. Quantum computers, on the other hand, use **qubits**, which can exist in **superposition** (both 0 and 1 at the same time) and can be **entangled** with other qubits, allowing them to process multiple possibilities simultaneously.

This ability to process information in parallel, combined with quantum algorithms like **Shor's algorithm** and **Grover's algorithm**, allows quantum computers to solve problems much more efficiently than classical computers for certain tasks. This is where quantum speedup comes into play: it allows quantum computers to outperform classical systems for specific types of problems.

Real-World Example: Time Taken to Solve Problems in Classical and Quantum Systems

To understand quantum speedup, let's consider a **real-world problem**: **factoring large numbers**, which is central to the security of modern encryption systems like RSA. Factoring large numbers is a difficult task for classical computers, especially as the numbers grow larger.

Classical Approach (RSA Encryption):

Suppose you are tasked with factoring a number that is the product of two large prime numbers, such as 300-digit numbers commonly used in RSA encryption. Classical computers use methods like the **general number field sieve** (GNFS), which is the most efficient classical algorithm for factoring large numbers. For a number with hundreds of digits, the time it would take to factor this number grows exponentially as the size of the number increases.

- **Time Complexity**: For a classical computer, factoring a 300-digit number could take **thousands of years** using the best known algorithms.

Quantum Approach (Shor's Algorithm):

Now, let's consider a **quantum computer** running **Shor's algorithm**, which was specifically designed to factor large numbers exponentially faster than classical algorithms. Shor's algorithm can factor large numbers in **polynomial time**, meaning that the time taken to factor a number grows at a much slower rate as the size of the number increases.

- **Time Complexity**: For the same 300-digit number, Shor's algorithm on a quantum computer could factor it in **hours** or **days**, offering a **massive speedup** compared to classical methods.

In this case, quantum speedup means that quantum computers can solve problems like factoring large numbers in a fraction of the time it would take classical computers, potentially breaking modern encryption systems.

Types of Problems Quantum Computing Excels At Solving

Quantum computing excels at solving certain types of problems that classical computers struggle with. Let's explore a few examples where quantum speedup offers a significant advantage.

1. Factoring Large Numbers (Shor's Algorithm)

As demonstrated in the real-world example above, **factoring large numbers** is a problem that classical computers find challenging, especially for numbers with hundreds or thousands of digits. Quantum computers, through **Shor's algorithm**, can factor these numbers in **polynomial time**, making them much faster than classical computers for this specific task. This has significant implications for **cryptography** and the future of secure communication, as many encryption schemes rely on the difficulty of factoring large numbers.

2. Search Optimization (Grover's Algorithm)

Classical search algorithms, such as **linear search**, require checking each item one by one in an unsorted database. For large databases, this becomes impractical. **Grover's algorithm**, a quantum search algorithm, can find a specific item in an unsorted database in $\sqrt{N}$ steps, where N is the number of entries. For example, if you're searching through 1 million items, Grover's algorithm can find the target in about **1,000 steps**, offering a **quadratic speedup** over classical search methods.

- **Real-World Example**: Searching for the best route in a traffic system, optimizing a supply chain, or looking for an optimal solution in a large set of possibilities are all types of problems where Grover's algorithm could provide a quantum speedup.

3. Optimization Problems

Quantum computers can excel at solving **combinatorial optimization problems**, where the goal is to find the best solution among a large number of possibilities. Classical computers often use **brute-force search** or **approximation algorithms** to find the optimal solution, which can take an impractical amount of time for large, complex systems.

Quantum computing algorithms, such as **Quantum Approximate Optimization Algorithm (QAOA)**, use quantum mechanics to explore multiple possibilities simultaneously, efficiently finding the best solution.

- **Real-World Example**: Optimizing traffic flow in a city, determining the best schedule for employees in a large company, or solving logistics problems like finding the optimal shipping route are examples where quantum optimization algorithms could provide a significant speedup.

4. Quantum Simulations

Quantum computers can simulate quantum systems much more efficiently than classical computers. Simulating the behavior of molecules, materials, and chemical reactions is an important task in fields like **pharmaceuticals**, **material science**, and **energy**. Classical computers can struggle to model quantum systems accurately, especially as the complexity of the system increases.

Quantum computers can directly simulate quantum systems using algorithms like the **Quantum Simulation Algorithm**, which takes advantage of quantum parallelism to model systems that would be impossible for classical computers to handle.

- **Real-World Example**: Quantum simulation could revolutionize **drug discovery** by accurately modeling molecular structures and chemical reactions, speeding up the process of developing new treatments and materials.

5. Machine Learning and Artificial Intelligence

Quantum computing can also offer speedups in **machine learning** and **artificial intelligence** by improving the efficiency of training algorithms. Classical machine learning algorithms require large amounts of data and computational resources, and the time it takes to train models grows rapidly as the data set increases.

Quantum machine learning algorithms, such as the **Quantum Support Vector Machine (QSVM)** or the **Quantum Neural Network (QNN)**, can leverage quantum parallelism and speed up the training process by exploring many solutions at once.

- **Real-World Example**: Quantum computing could be used to train machine learning models much faster, especially in areas like **pattern recognition**, **image processing**, and **data analysis**, where large datasets need to be processed and analyzed quickly.

Comparing Classical and Quantum Speedup: A Real-World Scenario

Let's consider a **logistics optimization problem**, where a company needs to determine the most efficient delivery route for a fleet of trucks. The classical approach would involve checking each possible route and evaluating its cost, a process that becomes computationally expensive as the number of routes increases.

Classical Method:

A classical computer would need to evaluate each route one by one, which is a **combinatorial optimization problem**. If there are **N** possible routes, the time taken grows exponentially as the number of routes increases. For a large number of routes (say,

1,000 possible paths), a classical computer might take a long time to find the optimal solution.

Quantum Speedup with QAOA:

Using **Quantum Approximate Optimization Algorithm (QAOA)**, a quantum computer could explore all possible solutions simultaneously in superposition and use quantum interference to amplify the probability of the optimal solution. This would allow the quantum computer to find the optimal route in significantly less time, especially for larger problems.

Conclusion

Quantum speedup represents a dramatic shift in the way we approach problem-solving. While classical computers perform calculations sequentially, quantum computers leverage the unique properties of quantum mechanics to explore multiple solutions in parallel, leading to **exponential** or **quadratic speedups** for certain types of problems. Quantum computing excels at tasks such as **search optimization**, **combinatorial optimization**, **quantum simulation**, and **machine learning**, all of which are essential for solving real-world problems in fields ranging from cryptography to logistics and healthcare.

As quantum computers continue to evolve, the potential for quantum speedup will unlock new capabilities and possibilities in various industries, helping to solve problems that were previously intractable for classical systems. In the next chapter, we will dive into the challenges of **quantum error correction**, ensuring that quantum systems can operate reliably and consistently as they scale.

CHAPTER 13

QUANTUM DECOHERENCE – THE QUANTUM CHALLENGE

Quantum mechanics offers enormous potential for solving problems that are currently out of reach for classical computers, but there's a major challenge that stands in the way: **quantum decoherence**. Quantum systems, by their very nature, are fragile and highly sensitive to their environments. The process of decoherence occurs when a quantum system loses its quantum properties, such as **superposition** and **entanglement**, due to interactions with the outside world. This chapter will explain the issue of decoherence, why it makes maintaining quantum states so difficult, and how researchers are working to overcome this challenge.

What is Quantum Decoherence?

In quantum mechanics, particles like qubits can exist in multiple states simultaneously, thanks to the principle of **superposition**. This allows quantum computers to process many possibilities at once, exponentially increasing their computational power. However, **quantum coherence**—the property that allows quantum systems to maintain superposition and entanglement—doesn't last forever. As quantum systems interact with their environment (such as air molecules, temperature, or electromagnetic fields), they begin to lose their quantum behavior, transitioning to a more classical state. This process is called **quantum decoherence**.

Decoherence is the loss of **quantum coherence**, and it marks the point when a quantum system collapses from a state of superposition into a specific state, such as 0 or 1 for a qubit, making it behave like a classical system. Once decoherence occurs, the quantum computer can no longer perform the calculations or solve the problem in parallel, and the advantage of quantum computing is lost.

Real-World Example: The Wet, Slippery Ice Cube

To understand how decoherence affects quantum systems, let's use a familiar analogy: imagine a **wet, slippery ice cube**.

- **The Ice Cube (Quantum System)**: Think of the ice cube as a quantum system in a **coherent state**—just like a quantum system in superposition, the ice cube is stable and can slide smoothly in multiple directions at once. You can imagine it gliding across a smooth surface with perfect control, just like a qubit in superposition holding both 0 and 1 simultaneously.

- **The Environment (Interactions)**: Now, imagine the environment as a set of rough, bumpy surfaces (e.g., a table with cracks or dust). As the ice cube starts moving, it interacts with the bumps and cracks on the surface, and this interaction gradually slows it down, distorts its path, and causes it to melt. The **slippery surface** represents the quantum system interacting with its environment, and the **melting ice cube** symbolizes decoherence. The ice cube becomes less stable and eventually loses its slippery properties, much like a quantum system losing its superposition and entanglement.

In this analogy, just as the ice cube cannot maintain its smooth, stable motion after interacting with the environment, a quantum system cannot maintain its quantum state (superposition) if it's influenced by external factors. The more the environment interacts with the system, the faster it loses its quantum properties.

Why is Quantum Decoherence a Challenge?

Quantum decoherence is one of the **biggest challenges** in quantum computing because it limits the amount of time a quantum system can remain in a coherent state. For quantum computers to work effectively, qubits must remain in superposition for long enough to perform calculations. However, the moment decoherence occurs, the quantum system loses its ability to explore multiple possibilities at once, effectively turning the quantum computer into a classical computer.

1. Sensitivity to the Environment:

Quantum systems are **extremely sensitive** to their surroundings. Tiny changes in temperature, electromagnetic fields, or even the presence of nearby objects can cause a quantum system to decohere. This sensitivity is a result of the very **fragility** of quantum states. Unlike classical bits, which are relatively stable, qubits exist in a probabilistic state and can easily be disturbed by even small amounts of interference.

2. Loss of Superposition:

Superposition, one of the most powerful aspects of quantum computing, is extremely delicate. As soon as decoherence sets in, the qubit loses its ability to be in a superposition of both 0 and 1. Instead, it collapses into one definite state (either 0 or 1), and the quantum computation process is interrupted. This collapse prevents the quantum computer from performing its parallel calculations efficiently.

3. Time Limits for Quantum Operations:

Quantum computers need to maintain their qubits in superposition for a sufficient period to perform their computations. However, the time window during which qubits remain coherent is extremely short—this is known as **quantum coherence time**. If the coherence time is too short, quantum algorithms cannot be executed effectively. In practical terms, this means quantum computers might struggle to solve complex problems or run quantum algorithms if decoherence occurs too quickly.

What Causes Decoherence?

Several factors contribute to decoherence in quantum systems. The most common causes include:

1. Environmental Interactions (Noise):

Quantum systems interact with their surroundings in ways that classical systems don't. These interactions—whether through vibrations, heat, electromagnetic radiation, or other environmental factors—can disturb the qubits. Even tiny fluctuations can cause decoherence, forcing the quantum system to lose its superposition state.

2. Measurement:

In quantum mechanics, the act of **measurement** is inherently tied to decoherence. When you measure a quantum system, the superposition collapses, and the quantum state becomes definite. This collapse is a form of decoherence. Quantum computers rely on manipulating quantum states without measuring them until the computation is complete, but any unintended measurement can cause decoherence and disrupt the process.

3. Quantum "Leaks":

Another source of decoherence is when a qubit leaks information to its environment unintentionally. This "leakage" often happens when qubits are not isolated perfectly or when quantum gates are imperfectly executed, allowing the qubits to interact with unwanted degrees of freedom in their environment.

How Can We Combat Decoherence?

Quantum engineers are actively researching ways to combat decoherence and protect quantum systems from environmental interference. Some strategies to mitigate decoherence include:

1. Quantum Error Correction:

One approach to addressing decoherence is **quantum error correction**, which involves encoding quantum information in a way that allows the system to detect and correct errors caused by decoherence. Quantum error correction codes create redundant qubits, allowing errors to be identified and corrected before they affect the computation. However, this technique comes with a significant overhead, as it requires many physical qubits to encode a single logical qubit.

2. Isolation and Shielding:

To reduce the impact of environmental interactions, quantum systems can be isolated and shielded from external influences. This might involve cooling qubits to extremely low temperatures to reduce thermal noise or placing them in specially designed environments that minimize electromagnetic interference.

3. Decoherence-Free Subspaces:

Some researchers are exploring the concept of **decoherence-free subspaces**, which involves encoding quantum information in a way that makes it immune to certain types of noise. By carefully selecting the states of qubits, researchers can design systems where decoherence does not affect the quantum computation.

4. Topological Qubits:

Another promising avenue is the development of **topological qubits**, which are more resistant to decoherence because they store quantum information in topological states that are less sensitive to local disturbances. These qubits are still in the experimental phase but could provide a more robust solution for building scalable quantum computers.

Conclusion:

Quantum decoherence is a significant challenge for the development of reliable and scalable quantum computers. The process of decoherence causes quantum systems to lose their delicate quantum properties, such as superposition and entanglement, and limits the time available for performing quantum computations. Overcoming decoherence is essential for building quantum computers that can solve complex problems more efficiently than classical computers.

In the future, continued advancements in quantum error correction, isolation techniques, and the development of new qubit technologies, such as topological qubits, will help mitigate the effects of decoherence. As researchers continue to develop methods to preserve quantum coherence, we move closer to unlocking the full potential of quantum computing.

In the next chapter, we will explore **quantum error correction** in more detail and how it helps quantum computers become more reliable and fault-tolerant, ensuring that quantum systems can scale to handle real-world applications.

CHAPTER 14

QUANTUM ERROR CORRECTION – FIXING QUANTUM MISTAKES

In the world of computing, **error correction** is crucial to maintaining the reliability and functionality of systems. Classical computers use **error correction codes** to detect and fix mistakes in data, ensuring that programs run smoothly without losing information. However, **quantum computers** are far more susceptible to errors due to the fragile nature of quantum states. Quantum error correction (QEC) is therefore a critical area of research for making quantum computers both **reliable** and **scalable**. In this chapter, we will introduce quantum error correction, draw comparisons to classical error correction methods, and explore the strategies used to make quantum computers robust enough for practical use.

The Challenge of Quantum Error Correction

In classical computing, error correction is typically straightforward. Bits, the basic units of classical information, are stable and can be checked for errors using established algorithms. However, quantum computers use **qubits**, which have unique properties like **superposition** and **entanglement**. These properties make qubits extremely sensitive to their environment, and even small disturbances (such as noise, temperature fluctuations, or electromagnetic interference) can cause errors. The core challenge in quantum error correction is preserving the **quantum information**—the delicate superposition and entanglement—while detecting and correcting errors.

To put it simply, quantum computers need to **fix quantum mistakes** without collapsing the quantum state or losing the advantage provided by quantum parallelism. This is where quantum error correction comes in.

Real-World Example: Classical vs Quantum Error Correction

Let's begin by comparing quantum error correction to **error correction in classical computer systems**. In classical computing, when an error occurs—such as a bit flipping from **0** to **1** or vice versa—error correction algorithms are used to detect and correct the mistake without compromising the integrity of the system.

Classical Error Correction:

- **Parity Bit**: One common error correction method is using a **parity bit**. In a simple system, the data is accompanied by an extra bit that indicates whether the number of 1s in the data is even or odd. If the data changes during transmission (e.g., a bit flips), the parity bit will reveal the error, and the system can correct it by flipping the erroneous bit back to the correct state.

- **Checksums and Reed-Solomon Codes**: More complex error correction methods, like **checksums** or **Reed-Solomon codes**, are used to detect and correct multiple errors in larger data systems, ensuring that the integrity of the system is maintained.

Quantum Error Correction:

Quantum error correction, however, is much more complex because it involves maintaining **quantum coherence** while correcting errors. Since qubits are not as stable as classical bits, directly ing quantum information to create redundancy (as done with classical error correction) is **impossible** due to the **no-cloning theorem**. This theorem states that it is impossible to create an exact of an arbitrary quantum state. Therefore, quantum error correction methods must use clever ways to protect quantum information without ing it.

How Does Quantum Error Correction Work?

Quantum error correction techniques rely on encoding quantum information in a way that allows for error detection and correction without directly measuring or collapsing the quantum state. This is achieved by **encoding a single logical qubit** (the qubit that represents the data we want to protect) across multiple physical qubits.

The main principles of quantum error correction are:

- **Redundancy**: A quantum bit of information is distributed across multiple qubits, creating redundancy.
- **Syndromes**: Errors are detected by observing **syndromes**—patterns of measurement that indicate a mistake without revealing the quantum state.
- **Error Correction**: Based on the syndrome, the quantum system applies an appropriate corrective operation to return the qubits to their correct state.

1. Quantum Error Correction Codes (QECCs):

Quantum error correction codes use **redundant encoding** to protect qubits from errors. Common quantum error correction codes include:

- **Shor Code**: One of the earliest quantum error correction codes, the **Shor Code** encodes a single qubit of information across 9 physical qubits. It can correct errors due to bit flips (X errors), phase flips (Z errors), and even combined errors (YZ errors).

- o **How it works**: The Shor code encodes the state of a qubit in a way that errors in any one qubit can be corrected by checking the other qubits. This allows the system to detect and fix errors before they cause decoherence.

- **Surface Codes**: The **surface code** is a more practical and scalable error correction code that uses a grid of physical qubits to encode a logical qubit. It is especially powerful because it can be implemented on real-world quantum hardware more efficiently than the Shor code.

- o **How it works**: In the surface code, qubits are arranged in a 2D lattice, and logical qubits are encoded in groups of physical qubits. Errors are detected using **stabilizer measurements** and corrected using a combination of quantum gates. Surface codes are highly fault-tolerant and are considered promising for future quantum computers.

- **Steane Code**: The **Steane code** is another quantum error correction code that encodes a qubit in 7 physical qubits. It can correct any error on one qubit and is part of the family of **error-correcting codes** used to protect qubits from noise.

2. Syndromes and Correction Operations:

Once a qubit is encoded using a quantum error correction code, errors are detected by measuring the **syndromes**. These are patterns of measurement that indicate which qubit (or qubits) is in error. The key to quantum error correction is that **measuring the syndrome does not collapse the quantum state** but simply reveals the nature of the error. Based on the syndrome, the quantum system applies corrective operations to restore the correct quantum state.

For example, in the surface code, if a qubit's state is found to have been flipped due to an error, the system applies a correction to flip the qubit back to its correct state.

Challenges of Quantum Error Correction

While quantum error correction is crucial for the success of large-scale quantum computers, there are several challenges that need to be addressed:

1. Overhead in Physical Qubits:

Quantum error correction requires a **large number of physical qubits** to protect a single logical qubit. For instance, the Shor code needs 9 physical qubits to encode a single logical qubit, and even more qubits are needed for more advanced codes like the surface code. This means that as quantum systems scale up, the number of qubits needed for error correction increases dramatically, creating a significant overhead.

2. Fault-Tolerance and Scalability:

Building large, fault-tolerant quantum computers that can correct errors efficiently is still a major research challenge. Quantum error correction schemes need to be implemented in a way that allows quantum computers to scale up to the millions of qubits required for practical applications. The cost in resources and time to implement these error correction techniques must be minimized for quantum computers to be viable.

3. Decoherence and Noise:

Even with quantum error correction, the effects of **decoherence** and environmental noise still pose significant challenges. Qubits are highly sensitive to their surroundings, and quantum error correction must work in tandem with efforts to isolate qubits from noise and maintain coherence for as long as possible.

Conclusion

Quantum error correction is a crucial area of research for ensuring that quantum computers can perform reliable and robust computations. While quantum systems are inherently fragile and susceptible to errors, techniques like the Shor code, surface codes, and syndromes allow us to detect and correct quantum mistakes. As quantum computing continues to evolve, these error correction methods will be key to building scalable and fault-tolerant quantum systems capable of solving real-world problems.

In the next chapter, we will explore the potential of **quantum communication** and how it utilizes the principles of quantum mechanics to create secure communication channels that are immune to eavesdropping and hacking, thanks to the inherent properties of quantum entanglement and superposition.

CHAPTER 15

QUANTUM HARDWARE – THE PHYSICAL REALIZATION

Quantum computing is not just a theoretical concept—it is a **physical reality** being actively developed by companies and research institutions around the world. While quantum algorithms and software are important, the hardware that powers quantum computers is equally critical. Building reliable quantum hardware requires overcoming significant challenges, due to the fragile nature of quantum states and the extreme conditions required to maintain coherence. In this chapter, we'll explore the various types of quantum computers being developed today, such as those based on **trapped ions** and **superconducting qubits**, and discuss the challenges of building practical quantum hardware.

What Makes Quantum Hardware Different?

Quantum computers rely on the principles of **quantum mechanics** to process information in fundamentally different ways than classical computers. Whereas classical computers use bits to represent information as either 0 or 1, quantum computers use **qubits**, which can exist in a superposition of states (both 0 and

1 at the same time). This allows quantum computers to perform many calculations in parallel, significantly increasing their computational power for certain tasks.

The main challenge in quantum hardware is that **qubits are incredibly fragile**. They must be isolated from external disturbances (such as heat, electromagnetic fields, and vibrations) to maintain their quantum states. At the same time, qubits must be manipulated and measured with extreme precision to perform useful computations. As a result, quantum hardware must meet specific requirements, such as:

- **Low temperatures**: Most quantum systems require very low temperatures to reduce thermal noise.
- **Isolation**: Qubits must be protected from environmental disturbances to avoid decoherence.
- **Scalability**: The hardware must be able to scale up to thousands or millions of qubits to handle real-world problems.

Real-World Example: IBM and Google Quantum Computers

Two of the most well-known companies in the quantum computing space are **IBM** and **Google**, both of which are actively developing quantum computers using different types of quantum hardware. Let's take a look at how these companies are approaching the challenge of building quantum computers:

IBM Quantum Computers:

IBM has been a leader in the development of quantum computing hardware, with their **IBM Quantum Experience** offering access to real quantum processors via the cloud. IBM's quantum computers primarily use **superconducting qubits** as the building blocks of their quantum systems. They have been working on improving qubit coherence times and building more stable quantum processors that can handle a greater number of qubits.

- **IBM Q System One**: One of IBM's flagship quantum computers is the **IBM Q System One**, a 20-qubit quantum computer designed for commercial use. It uses superconducting qubits and operates at **extremely low temperatures** (around 15 millikelvins, which is just above absolute zero). This system is housed in a sleek, hermetically sealed unit to protect the qubits from environmental interference.
- **IBM Quantum Roadmap**: IBM has announced plans to scale up their quantum processors, with targets of building machines with **1,000 qubits** in the next few years. Their goal is to enable **quantum advantage**—the point at which quantum computers can solve problems

that classical computers cannot solve in a reasonable amount of time.

Google Quantum Computers:

Google has been a major player in the field of quantum computing with its **Quantum AI** team and **Sycamore** processor. In 2019, Google made headlines by claiming to have achieved **quantum supremacy**—the milestone at which a quantum computer can perform a task that classical computers cannot perform in any reasonable timeframe.

- **Sycamore Processor**: Google's **Sycamore** processor is based on **superconducting qubits** and achieved quantum supremacy by solving a specific problem (sampling from a random quantum circuit) in just **200 seconds**, a task that would take the most advanced classical supercomputers around **10,000 years** to complete.
- **Google's Quantum Future**: Google is focused on improving qubit coherence times, error rates, and scalability. Their roadmap includes building larger quantum systems with thousands of qubits to handle more practical use cases, such as optimization, machine learning, and material science simulations.

These real-world examples demonstrate that significant progress is being made in quantum hardware, but there are still many hurdles to overcome before quantum computers become fully operational for a wide range of applications.

Types of Quantum Computers

Quantum computers can be built using various physical implementations of qubits. The two most common approaches are **superconducting qubits** and **trapped ions**, but there are several other techniques being explored as well. Each approach has its own set of advantages and challenges.

1. Superconducting Qubits

Superconducting qubits are one of the most widely researched types of qubits and are used by companies like IBM, Google, and Rigetti. These qubits are based on superconducting circuits that carry current without resistance.

- **How it works**: Superconducting qubits are created using tiny circuits made of superconducting materials that can exist in two distinct energy states (0 and 1). By using microwave pulses, these circuits can be manipulated to perform quantum operations.
- **Advantages**: Superconducting qubits can be fabricated using techniques similar to traditional semiconductor

manufacturing, making them potentially scalable. They also have relatively fast gate operations.

- **Challenges**: The major challenge with superconducting qubits is that they need to be operated at **very low temperatures** (close to absolute zero) to maintain superconductivity. They are also prone to **noise** and **decoherence**, which limits their usefulness in large-scale quantum computations.

2. Trapped Ions

In the trapped-ion approach, qubits are represented by individual ions (charged atoms) that are trapped using electromagnetic fields. These ions can be manipulated using lasers, allowing them to perform quantum operations.

- **How it works**: Each ion is controlled using laser beams that alter the internal energy states of the ion. These ions are held in place by electromagnetic fields in a vacuum chamber, and interactions between ions can be used for entanglement and quantum computation.
- **Advantages**: Trapped ions have extremely long coherence times and are highly isolated from their environment, which makes them relatively stable. Additionally, they are well-suited for **entangling** qubits over long distances.

- **Challenges**: The main difficulty with trapped-ion systems is **scalability**. As more ions are added to the system, it becomes increasingly challenging to control and measure them all simultaneously. Also, the process of moving ions and creating the necessary laser pulses can be slow.

3. Topological Qubits

Topological qubits are a relatively new concept based on the principles of **topological quantum computing**. These qubits store quantum information in the **braiding** of particles known as **anyons**, which are resistant to certain types of errors.

- **How it works**: Topological qubits take advantage of the special properties of particles in two dimensions, where information is stored in the topology (the shape) of the particle's world line, rather than in the particle's state itself.
- **Advantages**: The main advantage of topological qubits is that they are **naturally resistant to decoherence** and errors because the information is stored in the braiding of particles, not in the individual quantum states. This makes topological qubits potentially more stable and error-resistant.
- **Challenges**: Topological qubits are still highly experimental, and creating and manipulating anyons is a

complex task that has yet to be demonstrated on a large scale.

4. Photonic Quantum Computers

Photonic quantum computers use **photons** (particles of light) as qubits. These computers perform quantum computations by manipulating the properties of photons, such as their polarization or phase, to represent quantum states.

- **How it works**: Photons are passed through optical components like beam splitters and interferometers, where their quantum states can be manipulated. Since photons are naturally **immune to decoherence**, photonic quantum computers can operate at **room temperature**.
- **Advantages**: Photonic systems are relatively easy to scale, as photons can be easily transmitted through optical fibers and controlled with existing technology. They also have low error rates due to the robustness of photons.
- **Challenges**: The challenge lies in **entangling photons** and creating **precise quantum gates** that allow for large-scale quantum computations.

Challenges of Quantum Hardware Development

The development of practical quantum hardware faces several significant challenges:

1. Decoherence and Noise:

Quantum systems are extremely sensitive to their environment, and even small interactions with the outside world can lead to decoherence. Maintaining qubits in a coherent state long enough to perform calculations is one of the biggest challenges in quantum hardware development.

2. Scalability:

While small quantum systems have been successfully built, scaling up to thousands or millions of qubits is a major challenge. As the number of qubits increases, the complexity of controlling, measuring, and isolating qubits also increases. Achieving **scalable quantum systems** that can perform real-world tasks is one of the key hurdles to building a practical quantum computer.

3. Error Correction:

Quantum error correction is essential for building fault-tolerant quantum computers. As qubits are prone to errors, creating effective error-correction methods that do not require an overwhelming number of physical qubits is a major research focus.

Conclusion

Quantum hardware is the physical foundation of quantum computing, and while we have made significant progress in building quantum computers, much work remains. Different quantum systems, such as superconducting qubits, trapped ions, and photonic qubits, each offer unique advantages and challenges. Overcoming issues like decoherence, scalability, and error correction is essential for realizing large-scale, reliable quantum computers.

As companies like IBM, Google, and others continue to make strides in quantum hardware development, we move closer to unlocking the full potential of quantum computing. In the next chapter, we will explore **quantum software** and how quantum algorithms are designed to leverage quantum hardware for solving real-world problems.

CHAPTER 16

QUANTUM PROGRAMMING LANGUAGES

Programming a quantum computer is fundamentally different from programming a classical computer. Classical programming languages, such as Python or C++, are designed to manipulate bits, which are either 0 or 1. In quantum computing, however, the fundamental unit of information is the **qubit**, which can exist in multiple states simultaneously thanks to **superposition** and can be entangled with other qubits. This introduces new concepts, algorithms, and techniques that are unique to quantum systems. In this chapter, we will introduce **quantum programming languages**, focusing on **Qiskit**, a popular framework for quantum programming, and discuss how quantum programming differs from classical programming.

What Makes Quantum Programming Different?

Quantum programming languages are designed to work with quantum systems, and they must account for the unique characteristics of qubits. Some key differences between quantum and classical programming include:

131

- **Superposition**: Classical bits are either 0 or 1, but quantum bits (qubits) can exist in a superposition of both states at once. This means quantum programming languages need to be able to handle quantum states that are probabilistic, rather than deterministic.

- **Entanglement**: Qubits can be entangled, meaning the state of one qubit is directly related to the state of another, even over large distances. Quantum programming languages must support operations that create, manipulate, and measure entanglement.

- **Quantum Gates and Circuits**: Instead of traditional operations like addition or multiplication, quantum programs use **quantum gates** to manipulate qubits. These gates (such as the Hadamard gate, Pauli-X gate, etc.) are the quantum analogs of classical logic gates, but they operate in ways that take advantage of superposition and entanglement. Quantum programming languages must allow the creation and execution of quantum circuits composed of these gates.

- **Measurement**: In quantum systems, measurement is not simply the reading of a value, as it is in classical systems. When a quantum system is measured, it collapses into one of the possible states, and the system loses its superposition. Quantum programming languages need to handle this process and its implications for the outcome of quantum algorithms.

Because quantum mechanics is fundamentally probabilistic, the output of a quantum program is not a deterministic result like in classical computing. Instead, quantum programs typically run multiple times to gather statistics on the possible outcomes, as each run of a quantum algorithm may yield a different result.

Real-World Example: Qiskit

Qiskit is one of the most widely used quantum programming frameworks. Developed by **IBM**, Qiskit is an open-source platform that enables users to write quantum algorithms, simulate quantum circuits, and run experiments on real quantum computers. It is designed to work with quantum hardware and provide a user-friendly interface for quantum programming.

1. What is Qiskit?

Qiskit is a **quantum programming language** that allows developers to build and execute quantum circuits on IBM's quantum computers. It is built on Python, so programmers can leverage Python's features while working with quantum-specific functions. It provides tools for creating quantum algorithms, simulating quantum systems, and running experiments on actual quantum hardware.

Qiskit consists of several key components:

133

- **Qiskit Terra**: This is the foundation of Qiskit, providing tools for creating quantum circuits, scheduling, and optimizing quantum programs.

- **Qiskit Aer**: This part provides simulators that allow quantum algorithms to be tested on classical machines before running them on real quantum hardware.

- **Qiskit Ignis**: This part is used for quantum error correction, noise modeling, and analysis of quantum systems.

- **Qiskit Aqua**: Focused on applications of quantum computing, such as optimization, machine learning, and chemistry simulations.

2. How Qiskit Works in Quantum Programming

Qiskit allows you to create quantum circuits by defining qubits, applying quantum gates, and measuring the qubits to obtain results. Here's an example of a simple quantum program written in Qiskit:

```python
from qiskit import QuantumCircuit, Aer, execute

# Create a quantum circuit with one qubit and one
classical bit
qc = QuantumCircuit(1, 1)
```

134

```
# Apply a Hadamard gate to put the qubit in
superposition
qc.h(0)


# Measure the qubit and store the result in the
classical bit
qc.measure(0, 0)


# Use the Aer simulator to run the circuit
simulator = Aer.get_backend('qasm_simulator')
result = execute(qc, simulator).result()


# Get the measurement result
counts = result.get_counts(qc)
print("Result:", counts)
```

In this example:

- **QuantumCircuit(1, 1)** creates a circuit with one qubit and one classical bit.
- The **Hadamard gate** (H) is applied to the qubit, putting it in a superposition of states.
- The qubit is then **measured**, and the result is stored in the classical bit.
- The **Aer simulator** is used to simulate the quantum circuit, and the results are printed as a dictionary showing the probabilities of measuring each possible state (in this case, 0 or 1).

3. Running on IBM Quantum Computers

Once you have created your quantum circuit in Qiskit, you can run it on IBM's **quantum computers**. IBM provides access to quantum processors through the **IBM Quantum Experience**, an online platform that allows users to run quantum programs on real quantum hardware. You can submit jobs to IBM's quantum computers, track their execution, and analyze the results using Qiskit.

How Quantum Programming Languages Differ from Classical Languages

Quantum programming languages, including Qiskit, differ from classical programming languages in several key ways:

1. Data Representation (Qubits vs Bits)

In classical programming, data is represented using **bits**, which can be in one of two states: 0 or 1. In quantum programming, data is represented by **qubits**, which can exist in a **superposition** of both 0 and 1 simultaneously. This means that quantum programming languages must allow for the representation of qubits in superposition, enabling parallel computation.

2. Operations (Quantum Gates vs Logic Gates)

Classical computers perform operations on bits using **logic gates** (such as AND, OR, and NOT). Quantum computers perform operations on qubits using **quantum gates** (such as Hadamard, Pauli-X, and CNOT gates), which manipulate the state of the qubits in ways that take advantage of quantum properties like superposition and entanglement.

For example, while a classical **AND gate** takes two bits and produces one bit as output, a quantum **CNOT gate** (Controlled-NOT gate) takes two qubits and applies a conditional operation— flipping the second qubit (target) based on the state of the first qubit (control).

3. Measurement and Collapse

In classical computing, **measurement** simply reads the value of a bit without altering it. In quantum computing, **measurement** causes the collapse of the quantum state, meaning that a qubit in superposition (representing both 0 and 1) will collapse into either 0 or 1 upon measurement. This is a key aspect of quantum programming that does not exist in classical programming.

4. Parallelism and Probabilistic Outcomes

Classical programming languages are deterministic, meaning that for a given input, the output is predictable and fixed. Quantum programming, however, involves **probabilistic outcomes**. Since qubits can exist in superposition, quantum algorithms may yield different results each time they are executed, with the probability of each result determined by the quantum state of the system. This probabilistic nature requires quantum programmers to think in terms of **probabilities** and **statistical analysis** rather than deterministic results.

Challenges of Quantum Programming

While quantum programming languages like Qiskit make it possible to write and run quantum algorithms, quantum computing presents several challenges:

1. Quantum Noise and Decoherence

Quantum systems are extremely sensitive to noise and decoherence, which can disrupt quantum states. Quantum programs must account for these errors, and researchers are working on improving **quantum error correction** techniques to mitigate these effects.

2. Limited Quantum Hardware

Currently, quantum hardware is in the experimental phase and is limited in terms of the number of qubits and coherence times. As a result, quantum programming languages must also be designed to work with noisy, small-scale quantum systems, often requiring the use of simulators to test algorithms before running them on real hardware.

3. Complexity of Quantum Algorithms

Quantum algorithms are fundamentally different from classical algorithms, and designing efficient quantum algorithms requires a deep understanding of quantum mechanics. Quantum programmers must learn how to exploit quantum principles like superposition, entanglement, and interference, which are not intuitive for most classical programmers.

Conclusion

Quantum programming languages like **Qiskit** are opening up the world of quantum computing to developers, enabling them to write, simulate, and run quantum algorithms. While quantum programming presents unique challenges, it also provides the opportunity to solve problems that are beyond the reach of classical computers. As quantum hardware improves and quantum algorithms become more sophisticated, quantum programming will play a central role in unlocking the full potential of quantum computing.

In the next chapter, we will explore **quantum communication** and how it leverages the principles of quantum mechanics to create secure communication channels that are immune to eavesdropping.

CHAPTER 17

QUANTUM SIMULATIONS – THE KEY TO SOLVING REAL-WORLD PROBLEMS

Quantum computers have the potential to revolutionize many fields, from cryptography to artificial intelligence. However, one of the most exciting and impactful applications of quantum computing is **quantum simulations**. Unlike classical computers, which struggle to simulate quantum systems, quantum computers are naturally suited for simulating quantum phenomena, providing a powerful tool for solving real-world problems in fields like **physics**, **chemistry**, and **material science**. In this chapter, we'll explore how quantum simulations work and how they can be used to address some of the most complex challenges in science and industry.

What Are Quantum Simulations?

Quantum simulations are computations that model quantum systems, such as molecules, materials, or quantum fields, using the principles of quantum mechanics. Classical computers can struggle with these types of simulations because they cannot efficiently model the behavior of large quantum systems. For example, the properties of molecules are inherently quantum in nature, meaning they cannot be accurately simulated using classical methods without enormous computational resources.

Quantum computers, on the other hand, naturally operate using quantum bits (qubits), which can exist in multiple states simultaneously, making them ideal for simulating the behaviors of quantum systems. By utilizing **quantum superposition** and **entanglement**, quantum computers can simulate large quantum systems much more efficiently than classical computers, making it possible to solve problems that are currently intractable.

Real-World Example: Quantum Simulations in Drug Development

One of the most promising applications of quantum simulations is in the field of **drug development**. The process of designing new drugs typically involves simulating how different molecules interact with each other and with biological systems. Classical computers have been used for this task, but the complexity of the interactions between molecules makes it a challenging problem. This is where quantum computers come in.

1. Simulating Molecular Interactions:

Molecules are made up of atoms, and the behavior of these molecules is governed by quantum mechanics. Classical computers simulate molecular interactions by approximating quantum mechanical calculations, but this approximation is computationally expensive and inaccurate for large molecules or complex interactions. Quantum computers, however, can model these interactions directly, using quantum simulations that are exponentially more efficient than classical methods.

For example, a drug that interacts with a specific protein might need to be modeled in a quantum simulation to understand how it binds to the protein, how it affects the protein's behavior, and whether it has the desired therapeutic effects. Quantum simulations can accurately simulate these molecular interactions, potentially speeding up the drug development process and allowing researchers to test new compounds more quickly.

2. Accelerating Drug Discovery:

Currently, drug development is a slow process that involves testing thousands of compounds, often taking years to identify promising candidates. Quantum simulations could revolutionize this process by enabling **faster screening** of potential drugs. Researchers could simulate the behavior of thousands of different compounds, identifying the ones most likely to be effective in treating a specific disease without needing to perform costly and time-consuming physical experiments.

- **Example**: Quantum simulations could help develop drugs that target specific proteins involved in diseases like cancer or Alzheimer's. By accurately simulating how different compounds interact with these proteins at the quantum level, quantum computers could help identify the most promising candidates for further testing in real-world laboratories.

Quantum Simulations in Physics, Chemistry, and Material Science

While drug development is one important application, quantum simulations also have the potential to transform other scientific fields, such as **physics**, **chemistry**, and **material science**.

1. Simulating Chemical Reactions and Properties

Quantum simulations can be used to simulate chemical reactions and the properties of materials at the atomic and molecular levels. In classical chemistry, many reactions are too complex to model with high accuracy. For example, simulating the transition states of chemical reactions, which are crucial for understanding reaction mechanisms, is difficult with classical computers.

Quantum simulations, however, can model these transitions with far greater precision.

- **Example**: Quantum simulations can be used to understand **catalysis**, a process essential in many industrial reactions. By simulating how different catalysts interact with molecules, quantum computers could help design more efficient catalysts for producing chemicals and fuels, potentially making industrial processes more sustainable.

2. Exploring New Materials

Material science is another field that stands to benefit from quantum simulations. The properties of materials—such as superconductivity, magnetism, and conductivity—are determined by quantum mechanical interactions between atoms and electrons. Classical computers struggle to simulate these properties for large or complex materials, but quantum computers can model them directly.

- **Example**: Quantum simulations could be used to discover **new materials** with specific properties, such as high-temperature superconductors or advanced battery materials. These materials could have applications in energy storage, quantum computing, and other industries. For instance, quantum simulations might help identify new materials for batteries that are more efficient, longer-lasting, and cheaper to produce.

3. Understanding Quantum Phenomena

Quantum simulations can also be used to study fundamental quantum phenomena, such as **quantum phase transitions**, **quantum entanglement**, and **topological states of matter**. Understanding these phenomena could lead to new insights into **quantum mechanics** itself and help improve quantum computing hardware.

- **Example**: Simulating quantum phase transitions, which occur when a material undergoes a change in its quantum state (such as from a superconducting to a non-superconducting state), could lead to a better understanding of quantum materials and contribute to advances in quantum computing hardware.

Challenges and Limitations of Quantum Simulations

While quantum simulations hold great promise, there are still several challenges and limitations that need to be addressed before they can become a routine tool for solving real-world problems.

146

1. Noisy Intermediate-Scale Quantum (NISQ) Computers

The current generation of quantum computers is still in the **Noisy Intermediate-Scale Quantum (NISQ)** era, meaning that they are small and prone to errors. These quantum computers have limited qubits (typically around 50 to 100) and can't yet handle large-scale quantum simulations with the precision needed for practical applications. However, researchers are actively working on improving quantum hardware and error correction techniques, and NISQ machines may still be able to solve smaller problems or be used in conjunction with classical simulations.

2. Quantum Error Correction

As discussed in the previous chapter, **quantum error correction** is a major challenge. Quantum systems are highly sensitive to noise and interference, which makes it difficult to run long and accurate quantum simulations. Developing reliable error correction methods is crucial to unlocking the full potential of quantum simulations.

3. Scalability

Simulating large quantum systems, such as molecules with hundreds or thousands of atoms, requires an enormous number of qubits and gate operations. Scaling quantum simulations to these larger systems while maintaining accuracy and stability is one of the biggest challenges in quantum computing today.

Conclusion

Quantum simulations offer an exciting and transformative way to solve complex problems in fields like **drug development, chemistry, material science**, and **physics**. By leveraging the power of quantum mechanics, quantum computers can simulate quantum systems more efficiently and accurately than classical computers, opening up new possibilities for scientific discovery and innovation.

While quantum hardware is still in the early stages of development, and challenges like noise, error correction, and scalability remain, the potential applications of quantum simulations are vast. From revolutionizing drug discovery to enabling the development of new materials and advancing our understanding of quantum physics, quantum simulations are poised to play a key role in solving some of the most pressing problems of our time.

In the next chapter, we will explore **quantum communication** and how it uses quantum principles to create ultra-secure communication networks that are immune to eavesdropping and hacking.

CHAPTER 18

QUANTUM COMMUNICATION AND QUANTUM NETWORKS

In the age of digital information, ensuring the security and integrity of communication networks has become more important than ever. Traditional encryption methods, while effective, are vulnerable to future technologies like quantum computers. Quantum communication, however, offers a fundamentally more secure method of transmitting information, leveraging the unique properties of quantum mechanics to create communication systems that are resistant to eavesdropping and hacking. In this chapter, we will introduce the concept of **quantum communication**, explore real-world initiatives like **China's quantum satellite**, and discuss the potential of quantum networks to transform the way we secure communication in the future.

What is Quantum Communication?

Quantum communication is a type of communication that uses **quantum states**—such as **superposition** and **entanglement**—to encode and transmit information. The key advantage of quantum communication is its **inherent security**, thanks to the **no-cloning**

theorem and the principles of **quantum entanglement** and **quantum measurement**. Unlike classical communication systems, where information can be copied and intercepted without detection, quantum communication ensures that any attempt to eavesdrop on the communication will disturb the system, alerting the sender and receiver to the presence of an intruder.

At the heart of quantum communication is **quantum key distribution (QKD)**, a technique that allows two parties to exchange cryptographic keys securely. QKD relies on the fact that measuring a quantum system will inevitably disturb it, making it impossible for an eavesdropper to intercept the communication without being detected.

Real-World Example: China's Quantum Satellite

One of the most notable real-world initiatives in quantum communication is **China's quantum satellite**, **Micius**. Launched in 2016, Micius is the world's first satellite designed to demonstrate quantum communication over long distances. The satellite uses **quantum key distribution (QKD)** to securely transmit encrypted messages between ground stations, marking a major step toward the realization of global quantum communication networks.

1. How Micius Works

Micius uses **entangled photons** to establish secure communication channels. The satellite is equipped with a **quantum communication payload** that sends entangled photons to two ground stations in China. These photons are used to create a shared secret key between the stations, which can then be used for secure communication.

- **Quantum Key Distribution (QKD)**: When the photons are transmitted between the satellite and ground stations, the quantum nature of the photons ensures that any attempt to intercept the photons will alter their states, alerting the parties involved to potential eavesdropping.
- **Entanglement**: Micius uses the phenomenon of **quantum entanglement** to link distant photons in a way that any changes made to one photon will instantly affect the other, even across vast distances. This allows for secure key exchange between the ground stations, regardless of the distance between them.

2. Achievements of Micius

Micius has achieved several **milestones** in quantum communication:

- **Quantum Key Distribution over 1,200 kilometers**: Micius successfully demonstrated QKD over a distance of more than 1,200 kilometers between ground stations in China, setting a new record for long-distance quantum communication.

- **Quantum teleportation**: The satellite has also demonstrated **quantum teleportation**, where quantum information is transferred between particles without physically moving the particles themselves. This is a key step toward establishing **quantum networks**.
- **Global Quantum Network Potential**: With Micius, China has made significant progress in building the foundation for a global quantum communication network, potentially revolutionizing secure communication.

Micius is not only an experimental project but also a demonstration of the potential for **space-based quantum communication**. By using satellites to facilitate quantum key distribution, China is working toward building a quantum internet that could offer unparalleled security for communications across the globe.

Quantum Communication: Principles of Security

The security of quantum communication is built on fundamental principles of quantum mechanics:

1. No-Cloning Theorem:

The **no-cloning theorem** states that it is impossible to make an exact of an arbitrary unknown quantum state. This means that in quantum communication, if an eavesdropper attempts to intercept a quantum message, they cannot create an exact replica of the quantum state. This prevents **quantum eavesdropping**—any attempt to measure or clone the quantum state will disturb the system, revealing the presence of the intruder.

2. Quantum Entanglement:

Quantum entanglement allows particles to be connected in such a way that the state of one particle instantly affects the state of another, even if they are separated by vast distances. In quantum communication, this property can be used to establish **secure communication channels**. When two particles are entangled, measuring one will immediately affect the other, providing a way to detect interference or tampering.

3. Quantum Measurement and Disturbance:

In quantum mechanics, **measurement** of a quantum state necessarily disturbs it. This is a key feature of quantum communication: when information is transmitted using quantum states, any attempt to intercept or measure the quantum information will alter its state, allowing the sender and receiver to detect the presence of an eavesdropper. This makes quantum communication inherently secure—an eavesdropper cannot listen in on the communication without being detected.

Quantum Networks: The Next Step

While quantum communication over short distances has been demonstrated successfully, **quantum networks**—which connect quantum computers and quantum communication devices over long distances—are the next frontier. The development of global quantum networks will enable secure, encrypted communication on a scale never before possible.

1. Quantum Repeaters and Long-Distance Communication

One of the challenges of building a global quantum network is that quantum information degrades over long distances due to the **fragility of quantum states**. Quantum **repeaters** are devices that can help extend the range of quantum communication by amplifying quantum signals without measuring or disturbing the quantum information. These repeaters will play a crucial role in building a large-scale **quantum internet**.

2. Quantum Internet

A **quantum internet** would connect quantum devices over long distances, using quantum communication to enable ultra-secure communication, faster computation, and new capabilities for information sharing. In a quantum internet:

- **Quantum entanglement** could be used to link distant quantum computers, creating a **quantum cloud** that allows for distributed quantum computing.
- **Quantum communication channels** would be able to transfer quantum information securely between devices, ensuring privacy and protection from eavesdropping.
- **Quantum networks** could be used for new applications such as **secure voting systems**, **secure financial transactions**, and even **quantum-secure cloud computing**.

Challenges and the Road Ahead

While the potential of quantum communication and quantum networks is vast, there are still significant challenges to overcome:

- **Hardware and Infrastructure**: Developing reliable and scalable quantum communication hardware, such as **quantum repeaters** and **entangled photon sources**, is crucial for creating a large-scale quantum internet.
- **Integration with Existing Networks**: Quantum communication will need to be integrated with existing classical communication infrastructure, allowing for

155

hybrid systems that combine the benefits of both quantum and classical networks.

- **Noise and Decoherence**: Maintaining **quantum coherence** over long distances and dealing with noise and decoherence are significant challenges that need to be addressed before quantum communication networks can become practical for everyday use.

Conclusion

Quantum communication represents a major leap forward in the security and capability of communication networks. Thanks to the inherent principles of quantum mechanics, quantum communication systems are fundamentally more secure than classical systems, offering a new level of protection against eavesdropping and hacking. Initiatives like **China's quantum satellite Micius** demonstrate the growing potential of quantum communication and set the stage for the development of a global **quantum internet**.

As research continues, the challenges of scaling quantum communication systems will be addressed, leading to secure and efficient communication networks that will transform industries, from finance to healthcare to national security. In the next chapter, we will explore **quantum cryptography** in greater detail and how quantum key distribution is set to revolutionize cybersecurity by enabling ultra-secure encryption methods.

CHAPTER 19

THE QUANTUM INTERNET – A NEW FRONTIER

The **quantum internet** represents a monumental shift in how we communicate, collaborate, and secure our information on a global scale. Traditional communication networks, while powerful, face growing threats in the age of cybersecurity risks and the looming potential of quantum computers capable of breaking existing encryption methods. The quantum internet offers a radically different approach, relying on the principles of **quantum mechanics** to create ultra-secure, fast, and efficient communication systems. This chapter will explore the future of the quantum internet, its implications on global communication, and how it will revolutionize industries like **cybersecurity**, **cloud computing**, and **global networking**.

What is the Quantum Internet?

The **quantum internet** is a new kind of communication network that uses **quantum bits (qubits)** to transmit information instead of classical bits. It is based on the principles of **quantum entanglement**, **superposition**, and **quantum key distribution**

(QKD), allowing for ultra-secure communication channels that are fundamentally immune to eavesdropping.

Whereas classical networks transmit information through electrical signals or light pulses, quantum networks leverage the unique properties of quantum mechanics, such as **quantum entanglement**, to transmit information. **Entangled particles** can instantaneously affect each other, even when separated by vast distances, allowing for faster and more secure data transmission. The quantum internet would connect quantum computers, sensors, and communication devices over long distances, creating a **global quantum network**.

Real-World Example: The Quantum Internet and Cybersecurity

One of the most significant advantages of the quantum internet lies in its **potential to revolutionize cybersecurity**. With the rise of quantum computers, traditional encryption methods (such as RSA) that secure most of today's communications are under threat. Quantum computers can break these encryption systems much faster than classical computers, potentially exposing sensitive data to hackers.

Quantum Key Distribution (QKD):

Quantum key distribution is the cornerstone of quantum communication security. QKD allows two parties to share a cryptographic key securely, using the principles of quantum mechanics. The key idea behind QKD is that any attempt to intercept or measure the quantum communication will disturb the system, causing noticeable changes that alert the communicating parties.

- **Real-World Example – Quantum Key Distribution in Practice**:
  - In 2017, **China** launched its **Micius satellite**, which successfully demonstrated QKD between the satellite and ground stations. The satellite used **entangled photons** to distribute cryptographic keys securely over vast distances, marking a significant milestone in the development of a global quantum communication network.
  - **Quantum-secure communication**: QKD ensures that any interception of the key would immediately disrupt the communication, making it impossible for hackers to eavesdrop without being detected. This offers a level of security that classical encryption systems cannot match.

Implications for Cybersecurity:

As quantum computers become more powerful, traditional cryptography will be rendered obsolete. The quantum internet, with its reliance on quantum principles like QKD and **quantum entanglement**, promises to offer **unbreakable encryption** and **data protection**. For industries like banking, defense, and healthcare, where data security is critical, the quantum internet offers an **unprecedented level of protection** against cyberattacks and data breaches. Quantum encryption will safeguard the privacy and integrity of communications, ensuring that only authorized parties can access sensitive information.

The Future of the Quantum Internet

While the quantum internet is still in its infancy, researchers and companies around the world are working toward realizing its potential. Let's explore some of the key developments and future possibilities of the quantum internet.

1. Global Quantum Networks

In the coming years, **quantum repeaters** and **entanglement swapping** will enable the creation of large-scale, **global quantum networks**. These technologies will allow quantum communication to extend over long distances, including between countries and continents. The quantum internet will seamlessly integrate with existing classical networks, allowing for secure communication between classical devices and quantum systems.

- **Quantum repeaters**: These devices will act as intermediaries to extend the range of quantum communication by **re-generating quantum entanglement** between distant nodes. They will be essential for creating a quantum internet that spans large geographical areas.

2. Quantum Cloud Computing

One of the exciting possibilities of the quantum internet is the development of **quantum cloud computing**. In a quantum cloud, quantum computers and quantum resources are distributed across the internet, allowing users to access quantum computing power remotely.

- **Example – Cloud-Based Quantum Computing**: Companies like **IBM**, **Google**, and **Microsoft** are already offering access to quantum computing platforms through the cloud, allowing researchers and developers to run quantum algorithms on real quantum processors. The quantum internet will further expand the potential of cloud-based quantum computing by creating networks that interconnect quantum processors, facilitating **distributed quantum computing**.

3. Quantum-enhanced Internet of Things (IoT)

The **Internet of Things (IoT)**, which connects everyday devices like smart thermostats, cameras, and wearables, could be significantly enhanced by quantum communication. By using quantum secure communication channels, IoT devices can securely exchange data and perform quantum-enhanced tasks, such as processing quantum data or performing quantum-level optimizations.

- **Example**: Quantum-enhanced IoT could improve the security of critical infrastructure (like power grids or transportation systems) by ensuring that all communications between devices are encrypted with **quantum keys** that cannot be intercepted or tampered with.

Challenges and Roadblocks

While the potential of the quantum internet is immense, there are still significant challenges to overcome before it becomes a reality:

1. Technical Challenges in Quantum Hardware

Building large-scale quantum communication networks requires significant advances in quantum hardware. Quantum devices such as **quantum repeaters**, **entangled photon sources**, and **quantum routers** need to be developed to extend quantum communication over long distances.

Additionally, qubits are highly susceptible to noise and decoherence, making it difficult to maintain the **quantum states** necessary for secure communication. Advances in **quantum error correction** will be critical to ensuring the reliability of quantum networks.

2. Scalability of Quantum Networks

Creating a **global quantum internet** requires the integration of quantum communication systems with existing infrastructure, such as optical fiber networks and satellites. This is a huge undertaking, and creating a scalable and efficient network will require significant investment and collaboration between governments, businesses, and research institutions.

3. Quantum Cybersecurity Standards

As the quantum internet develops, there will be a need for new **quantum cybersecurity standards** and regulations. Governments and organizations will need to establish protocols for secure quantum key distribution, authentication, and data privacy. Additionally, quantum communication systems must be interoperable with existing classical systems to enable smooth integration and cooperation between quantum and classical networks.

Conclusion

The quantum internet represents a transformative shift in how we think about communication and security. By leveraging the principles of quantum mechanics, the quantum internet promises to offer **unbreakable encryption** and **unprecedented security** for global communication. The potential for **quantum key distribution** and **quantum-secure communication** could revolutionize industries such as finance, healthcare, and national security, providing a level of protection that is not possible with classical systems.

While there are significant challenges to overcome, the progress made by initiatives like **China's quantum satellite Micius** and the development of quantum repeaters and quantum cloud computing point to a future where the quantum internet will become a reality. As we continue to advance quantum technologies, the quantum internet will play a crucial role in securing our digital future and enabling new forms of communication, collaboration, and computing that were previously unimaginable.

In the next chapter, we will explore the **real-world applications of quantum computing** in fields like **medicine, finance**, and **logistics**, and how quantum technologies are set to solve some of the most pressing problems of our time.

CHAPTER 20

QUANTUM COMPUTING FOR MACHINE LEARNING

Machine learning (ML) has revolutionized industries by enabling computers to learn from data and make decisions or predictions without being explicitly programmed. However, as the complexity and volume of data grow, traditional computing methods for training machine learning models can become slow and computationally expensive. This is where **quantum computing** could play a transformative role. By leveraging quantum superposition, entanglement, and parallelism, quantum computing has the potential to **accelerate machine learning models** and solve problems that are currently intractable for classical computers. In this chapter, we will explore how quantum computing could change machine learning algorithms and its potential to enhance artificial intelligence (AI).

What is Quantum Machine Learning?

Quantum machine learning (QML) is a hybrid field that combines **quantum computing** with **machine learning** algorithms. The idea behind quantum machine learning is to use quantum computers to solve parts of machine learning tasks more efficiently than classical computers. Quantum computers can perform certain types of calculations much faster than classical systems, especially when it comes to operations that involve large datasets or complex mathematical models.

Quantum machine learning can potentially improve **data processing**, **model optimization**, and **pattern recognition** tasks by utilizing quantum algorithms and quantum properties like **superposition** and **entanglement**. These quantum properties enable quantum computers to process vast amounts of data in parallel, making them an ideal tool for training complex AI models faster than classical systems.

Real-World Example: How Quantum Machine Learning Could Accelerate AI Models

Let's explore how **quantum machine learning** could accelerate AI models, using a real-world example from the field of **image recognition**.

1. Image Recognition with Classical Machine Learning:

In traditional machine learning, a common algorithm for image recognition is the **convolutional neural network (CNN)**. CNNs are designed to process pixel data from images, learning to identify patterns, shapes, and features that correspond to objects (like cars, animals, etc.). The model is trained on large datasets, adjusting its weights and biases over time to improve accuracy.

While CNNs can be very effective, training them on large datasets (like those containing millions of images) can be computationally expensive and time-consuming. Classical computers need to process each image and calculate the weights through sequential operations, which slows down the training process. As the data grows, the task becomes even more challenging, and classical systems can hit their computational limits.

2. Quantum Machine Learning for Image Recognition:

In quantum machine learning, the idea is to harness quantum computers to **speed up the process** of training and running machine learning algorithms. For example, quantum computing could improve image recognition by speeding up matrix operations, which are fundamental to machine learning models.

In this case, a quantum algorithm could be used to **speed up the linear algebra calculations** that are part of the CNN's training process. Quantum computers can leverage quantum **matrix inversion** and **quantum Fourier transforms** to perform calculations much faster than classical systems. This quantum advantage could make it possible to train models on larger datasets in a shorter amount of time.

169

Moreover, quantum **feature extraction**—a technique used to reduce the dimensionality of data while preserving important information—could be enhanced by quantum algorithms. Quantum feature extraction uses **quantum states** to represent data more efficiently, allowing the quantum computer to identify the most relevant features in an image, speeding up the learning process.

- **Quantum Speedup in Training**: With quantum machine learning algorithms, a quantum computer could train an image recognition model **exponentially faster** by simultaneously processing large amounts of data, reducing the time needed for training. This could lead to real-time AI predictions, such as instant object detection in videos or images.

3. Quantum Data Processing and Optimization:

Another key advantage of quantum machine learning is its ability to optimize the training process. In classical machine learning, **gradient descent** is often used to minimize the error in a model's predictions by adjusting the weights. However, gradient descent can be computationally intensive, particularly for large datasets or complex models.

Quantum optimization algorithms, such as **Quantum Approximate Optimization Algorithm (QAOA)**, could be used to **optimize machine learning models** faster and more efficiently. Quantum optimization methods can explore multiple solutions in parallel, enabling the algorithm to converge to the optimal solution faster than classical methods.

For example, instead of evaluating potential solutions one by one (as classical algorithms do), quantum algorithms can evaluate all possible solutions simultaneously using **quantum superposition** and **entanglement**, speeding up the optimization process. This could result in more accurate AI models trained in less time.

Quantum Machine Learning Algorithms

Several quantum algorithms have been developed to help enhance machine learning tasks. Here are some of the key quantum machine learning algorithms:

1. Quantum Support Vector Machines (QSVM)

Support Vector Machines (SVM) are commonly used for classification tasks in machine learning. Quantum versions of SVM (Quantum SVMs) use quantum computing techniques to find the optimal separating hyperplane between different data classes. QSVMs can provide **exponential speedup** over classical SVMs, especially for problems involving large datasets.

171

- **Quantum Advantage**: Quantum SVMs use quantum processors to perform the kernel trick more efficiently, reducing the time required to compute the separating hyperplane. This allows for faster classification and better performance on complex datasets.

2. Quantum k-Means Clustering

Clustering is a common task in machine learning, used to group data into clusters based on similarity. The **k-means clustering** algorithm is widely used for this purpose. Quantum computing can enhance this algorithm by **speeding up the optimization** process and allowing for more accurate cluster identification in large datasets.

- **Quantum Speedup**: Quantum-enhanced k-means clustering uses quantum parallelism to evaluate multiple clusters simultaneously, resulting in faster clustering and improved accuracy in less time.

3. Variational Quantum Algorithms (VQA)

Variational Quantum Algorithms are a class of algorithms that use quantum computers to optimize a cost function while using classical computers for the variational part of the algorithm. This hybrid approach allows quantum computers to perform tasks like **model optimization** in machine learning more efficiently.

172

- **Example**: Variational Quantum Classifiers (VQC) are a quantum machine learning approach that uses both quantum and classical resources to classify data. These algorithms use quantum circuits to represent model parameters and classical optimizers to tune the parameters, combining the power of quantum computation with the flexibility of classical optimization.

4. Quantum Neural Networks (QNN)

Quantum Neural Networks are an extension of classical neural networks that use quantum gates and qubits instead of classical operations and bits. These networks aim to take advantage of quantum parallelism and entanglement to enhance neural network learning, potentially speeding up the process of pattern recognition and decision-making.

- **Quantum Advantage**: Quantum neural networks can process large datasets in parallel and handle high-dimensional data more efficiently, offering an exponential speedup in training times for deep learning models.

Challenges in Quantum Machine Learning

Despite its promise, quantum machine learning still faces several challenges:

1. Noisy Intermediate-Scale Quantum (NISQ) Hardware

Current quantum computers are in the **NISQ** era, meaning they have limited qubits and are prone to noise and decoherence. This makes it difficult to run large-scale quantum machine learning algorithms. Researchers are working on improving quantum error correction and building more stable quantum computers, but the hardware still has limitations.

2. Algorithm Development

Quantum machine learning algorithms are still in their infancy. Many of the algorithms we've discussed are still experimental, and more research is needed to develop **robust** and **scalable quantum algorithms** that can be applied to real-world machine learning problems. It's also necessary to create **hybrid quantum-classical systems** that can combine the strengths of both quantum and classical computing.

3. Data Encoding

Quantum computers require data to be encoded in quantum states, and finding the best methods for encoding classical data into quantum states is a challenge. Efficiently transforming large classical datasets into quantum formats is a key hurdle in quantum machine learning.

Conclusion

Quantum machine learning holds the potential to **accelerate AI models** and **revolutionize machine learning algorithms**. By using the power of quantum computing, we can solve problems that are currently intractable for classical computers, such as optimizing large datasets, improving model accuracy, and speeding up the training process. While quantum machine learning is still in its early stages, the potential to transform fields such as **image recognition, optimization**, and **data analysis** is immense.

As quantum computing technology improves and more quantum algorithms are developed, quantum machine learning will become a cornerstone of artificial intelligence, helping to solve complex problems faster and more efficiently than ever before. In the next chapter, we will explore the **real-world applications of quantum computing** and how industries are already beginning to benefit from these revolutionary technologies.

CHAPTER 21

QUANTUM COMPUTING AND ARTIFICIAL INTELLIGENCE

Artificial Intelligence (AI) has made significant strides in recent years, revolutionizing industries from healthcare to finance. However, despite its successes, AI faces inherent limitations, especially as the complexity and volume of data increase. These limitations primarily stem from the computational resources required to process vast amounts of information, train machine learning models, and optimize algorithms. **Quantum computing** holds the potential to significantly enhance AI by overcoming many of these constraints, speeding up learning processes, and improving efficiency. In this chapter, we will explore the synergies between AI and quantum computing, using real-world examples to highlight how quantum computers could address AI's current limitations.

AI's Current Limitations

AI models, particularly those based on **machine learning (ML)** and **deep learning**, have been incredibly successful at tasks like image recognition, language translation, and game-playing.

However, as AI systems scale up, several key limitations emerge that hinder further progress:

1. Computational Power

One of the most significant challenges faced by AI is the sheer **computational power** required to process large datasets and train complex models. Training a deep learning model often involves iterating over vast amounts of data, adjusting millions (or even billions) of parameters. This process can take days or weeks on classical computers, especially for large datasets like high-resolution images, videos, or unstructured text.

2. Data Processing Bottlenecks

As the volume of data grows, classical computers face **data bottlenecks**. In AI, models are often limited by the amount of data that can be processed at once. Classical algorithms, even though efficient in certain cases, struggle to keep up with the increasing demand for fast and parallel processing.

3. Optimization Challenges

Many AI tasks involve **optimization**, such as finding the optimal parameters for machine learning models or searching for the best configuration in a large solution space. Classical optimization algorithms, like **gradient descent**, are effective but can be slow and stuck in local minima. This becomes a significant issue in more complex AI problems where the search space is vast and highly multidimensional.

4. Model Efficiency

Current AI models require immense computational resources, including powerful **GPUs** (Graphics Processing Units) and specialized hardware. This makes training and deploying AI systems expensive and energy-intensive, limiting their accessibility and scalability for certain applications.

How Quantum Computers Could Enhance AI

Quantum computing has the potential to address many of these limitations by leveraging the principles of **quantum mechanics**— superposition, entanglement, and quantum parallelism. Here's how quantum computing can enhance AI:

1. Quantum Speedup in Learning Algorithms

Quantum computers can perform **parallel processing** on a massive scale, which could speed up the training of AI models significantly. Quantum systems can process many possible outcomes at once through **superposition**, allowing them to handle vast datasets and complex machine learning tasks more efficiently than classical systems.

For example, training a neural network traditionally involves adjusting the weights of millions of parameters using **gradient descent**. Quantum computers can enhance this process by leveraging **quantum optimization algorithms** to explore the solution space more efficiently. Quantum versions of optimization algorithms like **Quantum Approximate Optimization Algorithm (QAOA)** could reduce the time needed to find optimal weights, potentially speeding up the training process from days or weeks to just hours or minutes.

Real-World Example – Accelerating AI Training:

Imagine training a deep learning model for **image recognition**, where you need to process millions of high-resolution images. On classical computers, this task requires significant processing power, with the model taking several days to train. Quantum computers, leveraging **quantum parallelism**, could process all possible configurations of weights and biases in parallel, drastically reducing the training time. A task that once took days could be completed in just a few hours or minutes, enabling real-time AI learning.

2. Enhanced Data Processing

Quantum computers excel at handling large-scale, complex data due to their ability to represent and process information in **quantum states**. Unlike classical bits, which represent information as either 0 or 1, quantum bits (qubits) can exist in a **superposition** of both 0 and 1 simultaneously. This allows quantum computers to store and process exponentially more data in parallel, which is especially useful in AI tasks such as **image classification**, **natural language processing (NLP)**, and **speech recognition**.

- **Quantum Data Encoding**: Quantum computers can use quantum algorithms for **data encoding** and feature extraction. This would enable the efficient processing of **high-dimensional data**—a common issue in AI tasks, especially in fields like **genomics** or **drug discovery**, where the datasets can be vast and complex.

Real-World Example – Natural Language Processing (NLP):

In NLP tasks like **machine translation** or **text summarization**, the complexity of language leads to massive amounts of data that must be processed. Quantum computers can process these large datasets in parallel, allowing AI models to better understand and generate language faster and more efficiently. Quantum-enhanced NLP could lead to improvements in translation accuracy, sentiment analysis, and even human-computer interaction.

3. Quantum Optimization for AI Models

AI models often involve **optimization problems**—for example, finding the best parameters for a model or selecting the best feature subset in a dataset. Classical optimization algorithms, like gradient descent, can be slow and may not always find the global optimum, especially in highly complex problems with many variables and potential solutions.

Quantum computers can **accelerate optimization** by using quantum algorithms like **QAOA** or **quantum annealing**, which are designed to search large solution spaces more efficiently. Quantum computers can evaluate many possible solutions simultaneously and use **quantum interference** to amplify the probability of finding the optimal solution.

Real-World Example – Optimization in AI:

For instance, in **reinforcement learning (RL)**, the agent must explore and optimize its decision-making process by learning from feedback. Classical RL algorithms often require extensive training and exploration of many states before the optimal strategy is discovered. Quantum-enhanced optimization could speed up the convergence to the optimal solution, enabling RL agents to learn and adapt more rapidly in complex environments such as robotics or autonomous vehicles.

4. Quantum Machine Learning Algorithms

Several quantum algorithms have already been developed to enhance machine learning tasks. These algorithms leverage quantum mechanics to improve the speed and efficiency of learning processes.

- **Quantum Support Vector Machines (QSVM)**: Quantum support vector machines use quantum computing to perform classification tasks more efficiently than classical SVMs. They achieve this by using **quantum kernels** to map data points into higher-dimensional spaces, making it easier to find separating hyperplanes in complex datasets.

- **Variational Quantum Classifiers (VQC)**: VQCs use quantum circuits to perform classification tasks, leveraging the power of quantum parallelism to classify data faster than classical systems.

- **Quantum Neural Networks (QNN)**: Quantum neural networks utilize quantum circuits instead of classical layers to perform data processing. By leveraging quantum superposition and entanglement, QNNs can learn patterns and optimize their parameters much faster than traditional neural networks.

5. Accelerating AI's Learning Efficiency

Quantum machine learning could improve the **efficiency** of AI models, reducing the computational resources required for training. Quantum computers are particularly well-suited for training models with **high-dimensional data** or **large datasets**, which are often problematic for classical AI models. By enabling quantum-enhanced learning, AI models can achieve better results in less time, enabling real-time applications in fields like **healthcare**, **finance**, and **autonomous systems**.

Challenges in Integrating Quantum Computing with AI

Despite the promising synergies between AI and quantum computing, several challenges need to be addressed before quantum machine learning becomes mainstream:

1. Noisy Intermediate-Scale Quantum (NISQ) Hardware

Quantum computers currently operate in the **NISQ** era, meaning they have limited qubits and are prone to noise and errors. This makes it difficult to run large-scale quantum machine learning algorithms. However, researchers are actively working on improving quantum error correction techniques and building more stable quantum hardware.

2. Algorithm Development

Quantum machine learning algorithms are still in their early stages. Many quantum machine learning models are experimental, and more research is needed to develop scalable, efficient algorithms that can be used in real-world AI applications.

3. Integration with Classical AI Systems

For the foreseeable future, quantum computers will likely work in **hybrid systems** with classical computers. Developing efficient methods for integrating quantum algorithms into existing AI systems will be key to unlocking the full potential of quantum machine learning.

Conclusion

Quantum computing holds immense potential for enhancing artificial intelligence by accelerating learning processes, improving optimization, and enabling the efficient processing of large datasets. As quantum computers continue to advance, their synergy with AI will unlock new possibilities for solving complex problems in areas like **healthcare**, **finance**, and **autonomous systems**. While there are challenges to overcome in quantum hardware, algorithm development, and integration with classical systems, the future of AI-powered by quantum computing is incredibly promising.

In the next chapter, we will explore the **real-world applications of quantum computing** in sectors such as **medicine**, **finance**, and **energy**, highlighting how these technologies are beginning to make an impact across various industries.

CHAPTER 22

QUANTUM COMPUTING IN HEALTHCARE AND DRUG DISCOVERY

The healthcare industry, one of the most crucial sectors globally, stands to benefit greatly from the advancements in quantum computing. The potential applications of quantum technology in healthcare are vast and diverse, ranging from **improving diagnostic accuracy** to **accelerating drug discovery** and creating **personalized treatments**. In this chapter, we will explore how quantum computing is transforming the healthcare landscape, focusing specifically on **drug discovery** and **protein folding simulations**, while also discussing broader implications for diagnostics, treatments, and healthcare systems.

Quantum Computing and Drug Discovery

The process of **drug discovery** is long, expensive, and often fraught with challenges. Traditional methods rely on trial-and-error approaches, which can take years of research and billions of dollars to bring a new drug to market. A critical hurdle is understanding how potential drug compounds interact with complex biological molecules, especially proteins. Proteins are involved in nearly every biological process, and understanding how drugs can modify their behavior is key to designing effective treatments.

Quantum computing has the potential to **accelerate the drug discovery process** by simulating **molecular interactions** and **protein folding** with unprecedented precision and speed.

Real-World Example: Quantum Computing in Protein Folding

Protein folding is the process by which a protein molecule assumes its functional three-dimensional shape. Proper protein folding is essential for cellular function, and misfolding can lead to diseases such as **Alzheimer's**, **Parkinson's**, and **cystic fibrosis**. One of the biggest challenges in modern drug discovery is accurately predicting how proteins fold and how they interact with other molecules. Traditional methods of simulating protein folding are computationally expensive, especially for larger proteins with many thousands of atoms.

1. The Problem of Protein Folding:

Proteins are made up of long chains of amino acids, and their function depends on their shape. The folding process is highly complex because even small changes in the protein's environment

186

can significantly alter its behavior. Traditionally, scientists have used **classical computers** to simulate protein folding, but these simulations can be very slow and computationally intensive, particularly for proteins with complex structures.

2. Quantum Advantage in Protein Folding:

Quantum computers, with their ability to process vast amounts of data in parallel, offer a **quantum advantage** in simulating protein folding. Quantum algorithms can simulate quantum systems more efficiently than classical computers, capturing the nuances of molecular interactions at the quantum level. Quantum systems like **quantum annealing** or **variational quantum algorithms (VQA)** are specifically suited for optimization problems like protein folding, which involves finding the lowest-energy configuration of a molecule.

For example, **D-Wave**, a company specializing in quantum computing, has been using **quantum annealing** to solve optimization problems related to protein folding. By using quantum computers to simulate molecular interactions, researchers can understand how proteins fold faster, predict how diseases are triggered by misfolded proteins, and identify drug candidates that can help correct these misfoldings.

3. Quantum Computing and Drug Binding:

Quantum computers can also help simulate how potential drug compounds bind to target proteins. In classical drug discovery, researchers use a technique called **molecular docking** to simulate how small molecules interact with proteins. However, this process requires massive computational resources and is often slow.

Quantum computers could accelerate molecular docking simulations by leveraging **quantum superposition** and **entanglement**, which allows quantum systems to evaluate multiple interactions at once. This would enable faster identification of drug candidates and potentially reduce the time and cost required to bring new drugs to market.

Broader Implications for Healthcare: Quantum Diagnostics and Personalized Treatments

Beyond drug discovery, quantum computing has the potential to revolutionize other aspects of healthcare, including **diagnostics**, **treatment planning**, and **personalized medicine**.

1. Quantum Imaging and Diagnostics

Quantum computing can improve medical imaging techniques such as **MRI (Magnetic Resonance Imaging)** and **CT (Computed Tomography)** by processing data more efficiently and with greater precision. For instance, quantum algorithms can enhance the **signal-to-noise ratio** in imaging, resulting in clearer and more accurate images. This could lead to better detection of diseases such as **cancer, heart disease**, and **neurological disorders**.

Moreover, quantum technologies like **quantum sensors** can be used to create **more sensitive diagnostic tools**. These sensors could be used to detect minute changes in biological systems, enabling earlier and more accurate diagnosis of diseases, even at the molecular level.

2. Quantum Computing and Healthcare Optimization

Quantum algorithms can also be used to optimize various healthcare processes, such as **patient scheduling, resource allocation**, and **logistics management**. Quantum optimization techniques can help hospitals and healthcare providers make more efficient use of their resources, leading to cost savings and better patient care. For example, quantum algorithms could optimize the allocation of operating room schedules, the distribution of medical supplies, or the management of hospital beds.

3. Personalized Medicine

Personalized medicine, or **precision medicine**, is the practice of tailoring medical treatments to the individual characteristics of each patient. This approach requires analyzing large datasets, including **genomic data, clinical records**, and **lifestyle factors**. Quantum computing could enable the **analysis of these large and complex datasets** much faster than classical computers.

Quantum machine learning models could be used to identify patterns in patient data and predict the best treatment for individual patients. By simulating how different drugs interact with a patient's specific genetic makeup, quantum computers could help identify personalized treatment plans, leading to more effective therapies with fewer side effects.

Quantum Computing in Drug Discovery: Key Applications

Here are some key ways in which quantum computing is transforming drug discovery and healthcare:

1. Accelerating Molecule Design

Quantum computers can be used to model and simulate how molecules interact at the quantum level. By simulating the properties of molecules more accurately, researchers can design drugs that are more likely to bind to specific proteins or cellular targets. This can significantly shorten the time it takes to design new drugs and bring them to market.

2. Drug Repurposing

Quantum computing could also play a role in **drug repurposing**, where existing drugs are tested for new uses. By simulating the molecular interactions between existing drugs and new disease targets, quantum computers can quickly identify drugs that might be effective against other conditions, accelerating the search for new treatments.

3. Quantum Simulations for Toxicology and Side Effects

Quantum simulations could be used to predict how drugs will interact with various biological systems and how they might cause side effects. By simulating the interactions at the molecular level, quantum computers can help identify potential **toxicology issues** before drugs are tested on animals or humans, improving safety and reducing the need for costly clinical trials.

Challenges and Future Prospects

Despite the enormous potential, several challenges remain before quantum computing can fully realize its impact on healthcare and drug discovery:

1. Hardware Limitations

Quantum computers are still in the **Noisy Intermediate-Scale Quantum (NISQ)** era, meaning they have limited qubits and are prone to errors. The current hardware is not yet powerful enough to handle large-scale drug discovery tasks. However, advancements in quantum error correction and quantum hardware are expected to improve the performance and scalability of quantum computers in the coming years.

2. Algorithm Development

Quantum algorithms for drug discovery and healthcare are still in the experimental phase. Researchers are working on developing robust quantum algorithms that can be applied to real-world healthcare problems, but more work is needed to create scalable and reliable quantum models.

3. Integration with Classical Systems

Quantum computing will likely work in **hybrid systems** with classical computers for the foreseeable future. Developing methods for seamlessly integrating quantum algorithms with classical computing systems will be essential for real-world healthcare applications.

Conclusion

Quantum computing has the potential to transform healthcare by enabling faster drug discovery, improving diagnostic accuracy, and personalizing medical treatments. In the field of **drug discovery**, quantum computers can simulate complex molecular interactions and protein folding with greater precision, leading to **more effective treatments** for diseases that are currently difficult to treat. In the broader healthcare industry, quantum technologies could optimize medical processes, enhance imaging techniques, and enable personalized medicine, ultimately improving patient outcomes and reducing healthcare costs.

As quantum computing continues to evolve, its impact on healthcare will become increasingly profound, providing new ways to address some of the most pressing challenges in medicine and drug development. In the next chapter, we will explore **quantum computing in finance** and how it is set to revolutionize the financial industry by improving risk analysis, portfolio optimization, and market predictions.

CHAPTER 23

THE IMPACT OF QUANTUM COMPUTING ON CYBERSECURITY

As quantum computing advances, it brings both **opportunities** and **challenges** to various industries, particularly in the field of **cybersecurity**. While quantum computers have the potential to revolutionize encryption methods and data protection, they also pose a significant risk to existing cryptographic systems. Classical encryption methods, such as **RSA** and **ECC (Elliptic Curve Cryptography)**, are based on mathematical problems that are difficult for classical computers to solve. However, quantum computers can efficiently solve these problems, rendering current encryption schemes vulnerable. In this chapter, we will explore how quantum computers might undermine existing encryption systems and discuss the development of **quantum-safe cryptography** designed to protect sensitive data in the quantum era.

The Threat of Quantum Computing to Existing Encryption

Many of today's cybersecurity systems rely on **public key cryptography**, which uses two keys: one public and one private. These cryptographic systems ensure the confidentiality, integrity, and authenticity of digital communications. However, these encryption methods are based on mathematical problems that are challenging for classical computers, such as factoring large numbers or solving discrete logarithm problems.

1. RSA Encryption

RSA encryption, one of the most widely used public-key cryptosystems, relies on the difficulty of factoring large prime numbers. The security of RSA is based on the fact that classical computers would take an infeasible amount of time to factor large numbers used in the encryption process.

- **Quantum Threat**: Quantum computers, using **Shor's algorithm**, can solve the factoring problem exponentially faster than classical computers. Shor's algorithm can factor large numbers in polynomial time, breaking the security of RSA encryption in a matter of seconds or minutes, rather than years.

2. Elliptic Curve Cryptography (ECC)

Elliptic Curve Cryptography is another widely used encryption system, especially in mobile devices and applications requiring lightweight cryptography. ECC relies on the difficulty of solving the **Elliptic Curve Discrete Logarithm Problem (ECDLP)**, which is computationally hard for classical computers.

- **Quantum Threat**: Similar to RSA, ECC is also vulnerable to quantum attacks. Shor's algorithm can also solve the ECDLP efficiently, undermining the security of ECC-based encryption.

3. Symmetric Key Cryptography

While **symmetric key cryptography** (e.g., AES) is generally more resistant to quantum attacks than public-key cryptography, it is still affected by **Grover's algorithm**, another quantum algorithm that can search an unsorted database in **square root** time. In the case of AES, Grover's algorithm would reduce the strength of encryption by a factor of about $\sqrt{N}$.

- **Impact**: For example, if AES-256 (with a 256-bit key) is used, quantum computers could reduce the effective security to the equivalent of **128-bit security**. While this is still relatively strong, it may necessitate the use of longer keys (e.g., AES-512) to maintain security in a quantum world.

Quantum-Safe Cryptography: The Need for New Solutions

To address the potential risks posed by quantum computing to existing encryption methods, there is an urgent need to develop **quantum-safe cryptography**—cryptographic systems that are secure against both classical and quantum attacks. Research into quantum-safe encryption is already underway, with various approaches being explored to create new algorithms that will protect data in a post-quantum world.

1. Post-Quantum Cryptography (PQC)

Post-quantum cryptography refers to cryptographic systems that are designed to resist attacks from quantum computers while still being implementable on classical computers. PQC algorithms are being developed to replace vulnerable encryption systems like RSA and ECC.

- **Examples of PQC Algorithms**:
    - **Lattice-based cryptography**: Lattice-based schemes, such as **Learning With Errors (LWE)**, are considered strong candidates for quantum-safe encryption. Lattice-based encryption relies on the hardness of problems related to lattice structures, which are believed to be resistant to quantum attacks.

- o **Code-based cryptography**: Code-based encryption uses error-correcting codes to secure data. The **McEliece cryptosystem** is one example of a code-based cryptosystem that is considered resistant to quantum attacks.

- o **Multivariate polynomial cryptography**: This approach uses the hardness of solving systems of multivariate polynomials as the basis for security. These schemes are believed to be quantum-resistant.

- o **Hash-based cryptography**: Hash-based signature schemes, such as **Merkle signature schemes**, rely on the security of hash functions, which are also resistant to quantum attacks.

2. Quantum Key Distribution (QKD)

Quantum Key Distribution (QKD) is a quantum communication method that uses the principles of quantum mechanics to securely exchange cryptographic keys. QKD leverages the **no-cloning theorem** and **quantum entanglement**, ensuring that any attempt to intercept or measure the key will disturb the quantum state, alerting the communicating parties to the presence of an eavesdropper.

- • **Real-World Example – The Micius Satellite**:

198

- o China's **Micius satellite** is one of the pioneering efforts in implementing quantum communication and QKD over long distances. The satellite successfully demonstrated **entangled photon transmission** and key distribution between ground stations over 1,200 kilometers apart.
- o This represents a significant step toward secure global communication, as QKD ensures the privacy of the cryptographic key exchange, even in the presence of powerful quantum adversaries.

3. Hybrid Cryptographic Systems

As quantum-safe cryptographic systems continue to be developed, some experts believe that a **hybrid approach** could be the best solution for transitioning to the quantum era. In this model, classical encryption systems like RSA or ECC would be used alongside quantum-safe algorithms for a period of time.

- **Example**: A hybrid system could involve using quantum-safe key exchange algorithms (such as lattice-based systems) combined with classical symmetric encryption algorithms like AES. This would provide **dual-layered security**, ensuring that even if quantum computers can break one layer of encryption, the data would still be secure with the other layer.

Challenges in Quantum-Safe Cryptography

While the development of quantum-safe cryptography is underway, several challenges remain in making these systems ready for widespread use:

1. Standardization and Global Adoption

The development of quantum-safe algorithms is still in the experimental phase. Standardizing these algorithms, ensuring they are secure, efficient, and practical for real-world use, is a slow and careful process. Organizations such as the **National Institute of Standards and Technology (NIST)** are working on selecting and standardizing quantum-safe cryptographic algorithms, but it will take time for these standards to be adopted globally.

2. Transitioning from Classical to Quantum-Safe Systems

The transition to quantum-safe cryptography will require significant changes in infrastructure. Organizations must update their systems, software, and hardware to support new algorithms, and this transition must happen without disrupting existing services. This challenge is particularly significant for industries that rely on secure communications, such as banking, healthcare, and government.

200

3. Performance and Efficiency

Quantum-safe cryptographic algorithms must be not only secure but also efficient enough for practical use. Many of the promising quantum-safe algorithms are computationally more intensive than classical systems, which may lead to slower performance or require more processing power. Ensuring that quantum-safe encryption is scalable and efficient will be critical for its widespread adoption.

Conclusion

Quantum computing presents both **opportunities** and **challenges** to the field of cybersecurity. While quantum computers could break existing encryption schemes like RSA and ECC, they also pave the way for the development of **quantum-safe cryptography**. Post-quantum cryptographic algorithms, quantum key distribution, and hybrid cryptographic systems are all key components of securing data in the quantum era.

As quantum computing continues to evolve, the global cybersecurity landscape will undergo a significant transformation. Developing and implementing quantum-safe encryption will be crucial in protecting sensitive information from the powerful capabilities of quantum computers. In the next chapter, we will explore the **real-world applications** of quantum computing across various industries, highlighting how quantum technologies are already starting to make an impact.

CHAPTER 24

THE ROAD TO QUANTUM SUPREMACY

Quantum supremacy refers to the point at which a quantum computer can perform a task that is impossible, or at least impractical, for classical computers to achieve in any reasonable amount of time. This landmark achievement is a critical milestone on the path toward unlocking the full potential of quantum computing. In this chapter, we will discuss what quantum supremacy means, explore how it was achieved by **Google** in 2019, and consider the future of quantum computing research as we move toward more powerful and practical quantum systems.

What is Quantum Supremacy?

Quantum supremacy is a term coined by **John Preskill**, a theoretical physicist, to describe the point at which a quantum computer can outperform a classical computer at a specific task. It's important to note that quantum supremacy does not necessarily mean that quantum computers are more powerful than classical computers in all areas, but rather that quantum systems can solve problems that were previously **intractable** for classical systems.

A quantum computer can achieve supremacy when it uses quantum mechanical principles, such as **superposition** and **entanglement**, to solve problems faster than classical computers. The goal of quantum supremacy is to demonstrate that quantum computers can provide real-world benefits in specific applications, including **optimization**, **simulation**, and **machine learning**, that classical computers cannot practically replicate.

In 2019, **Google** achieved a significant milestone in this journey by demonstrating **quantum supremacy** in an experiment, making it one of the most talked-about achievements in quantum computing history.

Google's Quantum Supremacy Achievement

On **October 23, 2019**, Google's quantum computing team published a landmark paper in *Nature*, claiming that their quantum processor, **Sycamore**, had achieved **quantum supremacy**. In their experiment, Sycamore solved a specific computational problem in just **200 seconds**, a task that would have taken **10,000 years** for the most powerful classical supercomputer at the time, **Summit** (developed by IBM), to complete.

1. The Problem: Random Number Generation

To demonstrate quantum supremacy, Google selected a problem called **random circuit sampling**. The task involves generating a sequence of random numbers based on complex quantum circuits, and checking whether these numbers follow the expected statistical distribution. While the task itself was designed to be difficult for classical computers, it is relatively simple for quantum systems to solve due to the properties of quantum mechanics.

- **Why It's Hard for Classical Computers**: Classical computers rely on deterministic calculations to generate sequences of random numbers, but quantum computers use quantum circuits and superposition to generate much more complex distributions that are hard for classical systems to simulate accurately. Simulating such quantum circuits on classical systems requires an exponentially increasing amount of computational power as the number of qubits increases.

2. Achieving Supremacy

Google's **Sycamore processor**, which uses **53 qubits** (with one qubit intentionally unused to reduce errors), was able to process this random circuit sampling task in a fraction of the time that it would take a classical supercomputer. Google's claim of quantum supremacy came with a caveat: **Sycamore's achievement was specific to this one task**. While it demonstrated the power of quantum computing for solving certain types of problems, it didn't necessarily show that quantum computers are universally superior to classical systems.

However, the demonstration was significant because it proved that **quantum systems could solve certain problems** that were not practically solvable by classical computers—an essential first step in the journey toward more practical quantum applications.

What Does Quantum Supremacy Mean?

Achieving quantum supremacy is a breakthrough moment, but it's also just the beginning. Here's what it signifies for the field of quantum computing and the future of research:

1. Proof of Concept

Quantum supremacy demonstrates that quantum computing is no longer just a theoretical concept but an emerging practical technology. While quantum computers are still in the early stages of development, this achievement shows that they can outperform classical computers in specific tasks, paving the way for future quantum algorithms and applications.

2. Implications for Future Research

With quantum supremacy demonstrated, researchers can now focus on applying quantum computing to real-world problems. The next steps include developing **quantum algorithms** for practical uses in fields like **drug discovery, artificial intelligence, material science, cryptography**, and **optimization**. While current quantum computers are not yet suitable for most practical tasks, quantum supremacy provides the foundation upon which more complex and practical quantum systems will be built.

3. The Challenge of Scalability

While quantum supremacy was achieved using **53 qubits**, this is still far from the **millions of qubits** required for large-scale quantum computing applications. Scaling quantum systems is one of the most significant challenges faced by researchers today. Building large, stable quantum computers with low error rates and long coherence times is essential for realizing the full potential of quantum computing.

Future Directions: The Road Beyond Quantum Supremacy

While Google's quantum supremacy achievement is an exciting step forward, the road ahead for quantum computing involves overcoming several key challenges:

1. Error Correction and Noise Management

Quantum computers are highly susceptible to **quantum decoherence** and **quantum noise**, which can cause errors in computations. To scale quantum systems, it is crucial to develop advanced **quantum error correction** techniques that can mitigate these errors and maintain the fidelity of quantum computations over longer periods.

2. Building Larger Quantum Computers

Google's Sycamore processor, with 53 qubits, is just the beginning. To achieve practical quantum applications, quantum systems will need to scale to thousands, if not millions, of qubits. This requires innovations in quantum hardware, such as better qubit designs, improved error correction techniques, and new quantum circuit architectures.

3. Quantum Software Development

As quantum hardware advances, so must the software that runs on it. New **quantum algorithms** must be developed for real-world applications, and quantum programming languages (such as **Qiskit** and **Cirq**) will continue to evolve. Additionally, hybrid systems that combine classical and quantum processing will be key to making quantum computers practical for everyday use.

4. Integration with Classical Systems

While quantum supremacy demonstrates the potential of quantum computing, quantum computers will not replace classical computers. Instead, **quantum computing** and **classical computing** will likely work together in hybrid systems. Classical computers will continue to handle general-purpose tasks, while quantum systems will be used for specialized tasks that benefit from quantum parallelism and optimization.

Real-World Impact: What Does Quantum Supremacy Mean for Industries?

While quantum supremacy was initially demonstrated in a highly specialized experiment, its implications for industries are profound. As quantum technology matures, it will have far-reaching effects on several sectors:

1. Cryptography and Cybersecurity

Quantum computing's ability to break classical encryption systems like RSA means that quantum-safe cryptography is essential for securing digital communications. Researchers are already working on developing **quantum-resistant algorithms**, such as **lattice-based cryptography**, which will be needed to secure data in the quantum era. The implementation of **quantum**

key distribution (QKD) will also play a critical role in future cryptographic systems.

2. Drug Discovery and Healthcare

Quantum computing could dramatically accelerate the process of **drug discovery** and the development of personalized medicine. Quantum simulations will enable researchers to model the behavior of complex molecules and proteins at the quantum level, significantly improving the speed and accuracy of drug development.

3. Optimization in Logistics, Manufacturing, and Finance

Quantum algorithms have the potential to revolutionize **optimization problems** in industries like logistics, manufacturing, and finance. Quantum systems could solve complex optimization problems in areas such as supply chain management, financial portfolio optimization, and energy distribution, where classical methods struggle with scale and complexity.

4. Material Science and Artificial Intelligence

Quantum computing will also drive advancements in **material science** by simulating the properties of novel materials at the atomic level. This could lead to breakthroughs in **energy storage**, **semiconductors**, and **quantum sensors**. Additionally, AI models could be accelerated by quantum computing, providing faster training and more efficient learning processes for tasks like machine learning and natural language processing.

Conclusion

The achievement of **quantum supremacy** by Google is a historic milestone in the evolution of quantum computing. It demonstrates that quantum computers can outperform classical systems in specific tasks, providing proof of concept that quantum computing can be a transformative technology. However, quantum supremacy is just the beginning. The road ahead involves addressing critical challenges such as **scalability**, **error correction**, and **quantum software development**.

As quantum computing research continues to advance, we will see **quantum algorithms** applied to real-world problems in industries ranging from **healthcare** to **finance** to **cryptography**. The future of quantum computing holds immense promise, and achieving **quantum advantage** across more areas will be one of the defining technological achievements of the 21st century.

In the next chapter, we will delve into the **future potential of quantum computing** and the ways in which researchers and industries are preparing for the next wave of quantum breakthroughs.

CHAPTER 25

QUANTUM COMPUTING AND THE FUTURE OF TECHNOLOGY

Quantum computing is poised to redefine the technology landscape as we know it. It is not just an evolution of current computing models; it is a revolution in how we approach problems that are beyond the reach of classical systems. As quantum computers mature, they will bring about profound changes in industries ranging from **cloud computing** and the **Internet of Things (IoT)** to **artificial intelligence**, **medicine**, and **cryptography**. This chapter explores the potential impacts of quantum computing on these emerging technologies and offers a glimpse into the future of tech as quantum computing becomes mainstream.

The Role of Quantum Computing in Cloud Computing

Cloud computing has transformed how we store, process, and access data, providing on-demand resources through centralized servers. As more businesses and individuals rely on cloud services for their computing needs, the demand for greater computational power and efficiency continues to grow. However, there are limitations to what classical cloud systems can achieve, especially when it comes to **complex simulations**, **optimization problems**, and **machine learning** tasks.

1. Quantum Cloud Computing: Merging Classical and Quantum Systems

Quantum cloud computing refers to the integration of quantum computing resources with classical cloud infrastructure. This hybrid model allows users to access quantum computers through cloud platforms while continuing to rely on classical systems for everyday computing tasks. Companies like **IBM**, **Google**, and **Microsoft** are already working on **quantum cloud platforms**, enabling users to run quantum algorithms on real quantum machines remotely, using cloud-based interfaces.

- **Real-World Example – IBM Quantum Experience**: IBM's **Quantum Experience** allows users to access quantum computing resources through the cloud, providing an accessible platform for researchers, developers, and companies to experiment with quantum algorithms. IBM also offers its **Qiskit** software toolkit, which lets users write quantum algorithms and run them on IBM's quantum hardware over the cloud.

2. Accelerating Cloud-Based AI and Machine Learning

Quantum computing will dramatically accelerate the processing speed for **cloud-based AI and machine learning** applications. Classical machine learning models require immense computational resources to process large datasets and train complex models. Quantum computers can provide **quantum speedup** by solving optimization problems exponentially faster than classical systems, which will allow AI models to learn faster, predict more accurately, and handle more complex datasets in real-time.

For example, **quantum-enhanced machine learning** (QML) can optimize model training by leveraging quantum algorithms that handle high-dimensional data much more efficiently than classical algorithms. The ability to run such algorithms on quantum cloud platforms will make advanced AI capabilities more accessible, with applications in fields like healthcare, finance, and autonomous driving.

3. Enhancing Cloud Security with Quantum Cryptography

Quantum computing also has significant implications for **cloud security**. As mentioned in previous chapters, quantum computers can break current cryptographic systems like RSA and ECC. However, they also enable **quantum-safe cryptography** and

quantum key distribution (QKD), which can secure cloud communications with unbreakable encryption.

Cloud service providers will need to incorporate quantum-safe encryption methods to ensure that data remains secure as quantum technology progresses. Additionally, **quantum key distribution** will allow users to securely exchange encryption keys over quantum communication channels, ensuring that sensitive data remains private and protected against quantum-enabled cyberattacks.

The Impact of Quantum Computing on the Internet of Things (IoT)

The **Internet of Things (IoT)** refers to the vast network of interconnected devices, sensors, and objects that communicate with each other over the internet. As the IoT expands, the number of connected devices and the amount of data generated continues to grow exponentially. This presents challenges in terms of data processing, storage, and security, which quantum computing has the potential to address.

1. Quantum IoT: Enhancing Device Communication

Quantum computing can significantly improve the communication and efficiency of IoT devices. **Quantum sensors** have the potential to enable more **precise measurements** and improve the detection capabilities of IoT devices. These sensors use quantum principles like **superposition** and **entanglement** to enhance sensitivity and accuracy, allowing IoT devices to make more informed decisions and provide real-time data in **smart cities**, **industrial automation**, and **healthcare**.

For example, **quantum-enhanced sensors** could monitor environmental factors with unparalleled precision, helping industries better understand energy usage, pollution levels, or supply chain optimization. In **healthcare**, quantum sensors could detect biomarkers at much lower concentrations, leading to faster diagnostics and more personalized treatments.

2. Quantum-Powered Edge Computing for IoT

One of the challenges with IoT systems is the sheer volume of data generated by connected devices, often requiring real-time processing and analysis. **Edge computing** addresses this issue by processing data closer to the source, reducing latency and bandwidth requirements. Quantum computers could enhance edge computing by enabling **quantum-enhanced data processing** at the edge of the network, providing faster insights and decision-making capabilities for IoT devices.

- **Example**: In **smart cities**, where thousands of sensors collect data on traffic flow, energy usage, and environmental conditions, quantum-enhanced edge devices could process this data instantly and optimize city-wide operations in real-time, such as adjusting traffic lights, optimizing energy consumption, or predicting and preventing system failures.

3. Quantum Security for IoT

As the number of connected devices grows, so does the potential for security vulnerabilities. **Quantum cryptography** could enhance the security of IoT networks by enabling secure communication channels between devices. Traditional encryption methods may no longer be sufficient to protect IoT devices from quantum-enabled threats, but quantum key distribution (QKD) could be used to secure data transmission and ensure that IoT systems are protected against future quantum hacking techniques.

The Future of Quantum Computing: Beyond Cloud and IoT

The potential applications of quantum computing are not limited to cloud computing and IoT. As quantum technology continues to evolve, its impact will ripple across various other sectors, including **medicine, finance, material science**, and **artificial intelligence**.

1. Quantum Computing in Medicine

In healthcare, quantum computing will revolutionize areas like **drug discovery**, **personalized medicine**, and **genomics**. Quantum simulations will allow researchers to model complex biological processes, accelerating the development of new drugs and treatments. Quantum computers could analyze genomic data faster, enabling doctors to tailor treatments to individual genetic profiles and significantly improving patient outcomes.

2. Quantum Computing in Finance

In the financial industry, quantum computing could transform tasks like **portfolio optimization**, **risk analysis**, and **fraud detection**. Quantum algorithms can handle complex optimization problems much more efficiently than classical systems, enabling financial institutions to make better investment decisions, reduce risk, and detect fraudulent activities faster.

3. Quantum Computing in Material Science

Quantum computers could also revolutionize **material science** by simulating the properties of materials at the atomic and molecular levels. This could lead to breakthroughs in areas like **energy storage**, **superconductors**, and **semiconductors**, which would have wide-reaching applications in electronics, batteries, and renewable energy technologies.

Challenges Ahead and the Path Forward

While the potential of quantum computing is immense, there are still significant challenges to overcome before these technologies can be fully integrated into cloud computing and IoT systems.

- **Quantum Hardware Development**: Building stable, scalable quantum computers with low error rates is one of the biggest hurdles for quantum computing. Current systems are in the **Noisy Intermediate-Scale Quantum (NISQ)** era, meaning they are not yet capable of solving large-scale problems.

- **Algorithm Development**: Quantum algorithms for real-world applications in cloud computing, IoT, and other industries are still in the early stages of development. More research is needed to develop efficient and practical quantum algorithms that can be deployed at scale.

- **Integration with Existing Infrastructure**: Quantum computing will need to be integrated with existing classical systems, requiring new hybrid architectures that combine quantum and classical processing power.

Conclusion

Quantum computing holds transformative potential for the **future of technology,** especially in fields like **cloud computing, IoT, medicine,** and **finance.** Its ability to process data in parallel and solve complex problems exponentially faster than classical computers will reshape the tech landscape, enabling new capabilities and efficiencies. As quantum computers continue to evolve, we can expect to see a seamless integration of quantum and classical technologies that will unlock innovations across various industries.

In the next chapter, we will explore the **ethical implications** of quantum computing and discuss the potential societal impacts as these technologies become more integrated into everyday life.

CHAPTER 26

THE ETHICS AND CHALLENGES OF QUANTUM COMPUTING

As quantum computing continues to evolve and make its way into real-world applications, it brings with it not only groundbreaking technological advances but also a set of profound **ethical dilemmas** and **challenges**. The very nature of quantum computing, which promises to solve complex problems in fields ranging from **healthcare** to **cryptography** to **artificial intelligence**, raises important questions about its potential for both positive and negative societal impact. In this chapter, we will discuss the ethical implications of quantum computing, particularly in areas such as **surveillance**, **privacy**, and **security**, and the challenges that come with its rapid advancement.

Ethical Concerns in Quantum Computing's Applications

1. Quantum Computing in Surveillance

One of the most significant ethical concerns surrounding quantum computing is its potential use in **surveillance**. Quantum computers have the potential to break the cryptographic systems currently in use to secure private communications and personal data. While this capability could be used to improve security, it also presents the possibility for unprecedented **surveillance** capabilities, where governments, corporations, or malicious actors could exploit quantum technology to eavesdrop on encrypted communications, track individuals, and gather sensitive information.

Real-World Example: The Ethical Dilemma of Quantum-Safe Encryption in Surveillance

Imagine a future scenario where governments or intelligence agencies have access to quantum computers capable of **decrypting previously secure communications**. This raises a fundamental question: **Who controls access to quantum encryption-breaking technologies?**

- **Government Surveillance**: Governments could potentially use quantum computers to decrypt data transmitted through secure channels, raising concerns about the mass collection of private data, intrusion into citizens' lives, and violations of privacy. A state with access to quantum decryption tools could, theoretically, monitor communications, track individuals' movements, and infiltrate private discussions—raising questions about **surveillance overreach** and the **erosion of civil liberties**.
- **Corporate Surveillance**: On the other hand, private corporations could potentially use quantum technologies

for **targeted surveillance** and **data mining** on an unprecedented scale. By decrypting sensitive personal information, businesses could gain access to highly private data, such as personal communications, financial details, and even healthcare information, leading to concerns about **data exploitation**, **privacy violations**, and **consumer manipulation**.

2. Surveillance and Privacy Violations: Potential Scenarios

Quantum computing's ability to decrypt strong encryption will significantly affect **privacy** and **data protection**. **End-to-end encryption**—a key mechanism used by services like WhatsApp, email providers, and banks to protect users' data—relies on the difficulty of certain mathematical problems (e.g., factorization of large numbers) that are currently unsolvable by classical computers. Quantum computers, with the ability to quickly solve these problems, will undermine the **confidentiality** of encrypted data.

- **Scenario 1: Mass Surveillance Systems**
  In a world with quantum decryption capabilities, governments could monitor online communications on a massive scale. For instance, an authoritarian government could use quantum computers to decrypt communications between activists, journalists, and opposition leaders, suppressing dissent and violating privacy on a vast scale.

223

- **Scenario 2: Data Harvesting by Corporations** Companies could potentially gain access to consumer data that was once thought secure. For example, a company might decrypt personal communications or transactions to build detailed profiles of individuals, which could be used for **manipulating consumer behavior**, **targeted advertising**, or even **political influence**.

3. Balancing Security and Privacy

The rise of quantum computing places society at a crossroads: we need to balance **advancements in security** with the protection of **individual privacy**. While quantum computing could dramatically improve security protocols—such as in **quantum key distribution** for secure communications—it also poses a grave risk to privacy. This dichotomy raises ethical questions about the **right to privacy** versus the **right to security**.

Ethical Implications in Quantum Computing Research

In addition to its potential applications, quantum computing itself presents unique **ethical challenges** in terms of research, development, and access.

1. Access and Control of Quantum Technology

As quantum computing progresses, questions arise regarding who **controls** access to quantum technologies. The development of quantum computers is an expensive and complex process, which means that access to these systems may be limited to a few governments, corporations, or research institutions. This concentration of power could exacerbate inequalities in technological access and create **imbalances of power**.

- **Concentration of Power**: Countries or entities with access to quantum computing could gain a competitive advantage in **security, military capabilities**, and **financial systems**, potentially leading to geopolitical imbalances and widening the **digital divide**. Moreover, the power to decrypt and control communications could become a tool of **economic or political leverage**.

- **Fair Distribution of Resources**: The global community must decide how quantum technologies will be made accessible. **International agreements** may be needed to ensure that quantum computing is not monopolized and that its benefits are distributed fairly, especially in areas such as **healthcare, education**, and **scientific discovery**.

2. AI and Quantum Computing: A Double-Edged Sword

The convergence of **quantum computing** and **artificial intelligence (AI)** introduces a set of ethical concerns. On one hand, quantum computing could enable faster, more efficient **machine learning** algorithms, leading to breakthroughs in **medicine, science**, and **industry**. On the other hand, it could accelerate the development of AI technologies that could outpace our ability to regulate and control them.

- **AI Governance**: Quantum-enhanced AI algorithms may lead to more **powerful decision-making systems** in everything from **finance** to **autonomous vehicles** to **surveillance**. This raises questions about accountability, transparency, and control over autonomous AI systems that could make important decisions without human oversight.

- **AI Bias and Ethical Concerns**: The use of quantum computing in AI could also amplify **bias** and **discrimination**. Faster and more efficient AI algorithms could process data at a scale that magnifies existing societal biases, leading to AI systems that reinforce stereotypes or inequalities. Developers will need to ensure that quantum-powered AI remains **ethically aligned** with human values and is transparent and accountable.

Challenges in Quantum Computing Development

While quantum computing promises incredible advancements, there are several **practical challenges** that must be addressed before quantum technology can be fully integrated into society:

1. Quantum Computing as a Double-Edged Sword

Quantum computers will undoubtedly have a **positive impact** in areas like **medicine, energy,** and **cryptography**. However, as we've discussed, they also present challenges in **cybersecurity, privacy,** and **accessibility**. The ethical implications of quantum computing will depend largely on how governments, industries, and organizations choose to **regulate** and **control** the use of quantum technology.

2. Potential for Weaponization

The potential of quantum computing to break encryption and infiltrate secure communication networks raises the possibility of **weaponization**. A quantum-enabled nation or group could potentially launch **cyber-attacks** using quantum computers to steal sensitive data, infiltrate systems, or even disrupt critical infrastructure. This necessitates strict regulations, oversight, and **international agreements** on the use of quantum technology in military and defense applications.

3. Ensuring Inclusivity in Development

Quantum computing is a highly specialized field requiring significant investment in both **research** and **infrastructure**. As such, there is a risk that only a small number of wealthy nations and corporations will dominate quantum technology development, leaving others behind. It will be important to ensure that **developing countries** have access to quantum computing resources and can participate in the global research effort.

Conclusion

The ethical challenges posed by quantum computing are complex and multifaceted. While quantum computing holds the potential to revolutionize fields ranging from **healthcare** to **cryptography**, it also raises important questions about **privacy**, **security**, and **power dynamics**. The potential for **mass surveillance**, **data manipulation**, and **geopolitical imbalance** underscores the need for ethical oversight in the development and deployment of quantum technologies.

As we move forward, it will be essential to establish **global frameworks** and **ethical guidelines** that govern the use of quantum computing. These regulations will need to balance the promise of quantum technology with the protection of fundamental rights and freedoms. The decisions we make today

228

about quantum computing will shape the future of technology, privacy, and security for generations to come.

In the next chapter, we will explore the **future of quantum computing** and its long-term impact on industries, societies, and our daily lives.

CHAPTER 27

GETTING STARTED WITH QUANTUM COMPUTING

Quantum computing is no longer just a futuristic concept; it is an exciting and rapidly growing field that is becoming increasingly accessible to individuals and businesses. As quantum technologies evolve, beginners can now explore this powerful technology through **online platforms**, **open-source tools**, and **quantum simulators**. In this chapter, we will provide practical advice on how to get started with quantum computing today, using real-world examples like **IBM Q Experience** to help you dive into the world of quantum programming.

Understanding the Basics Before You Begin

Before diving into quantum programming, it's important to have a solid understanding of some foundational concepts. Here are the core ideas you should familiarize yourself with:

1. Qubits and Superposition

Quantum computers operate using **quantum bits**, or **qubits**, which are different from classical bits. While classical bits can be either **0** or **1**, qubits can exist in **superposition**, meaning they can be in multiple states at once (both 0 and 1). This property allows quantum computers to process much more information in parallel than classical systems.

2. Quantum Gates

In quantum computing, operations are performed using **quantum gates**—mathematical operations that manipulate qubits. Quantum gates function similarly to classical logic gates (such as AND, OR, and NOT gates), but they work according to the principles of quantum mechanics.

3. Quantum Entanglement

Quantum entanglement is a phenomenon where qubits become correlated in such a way that the state of one qubit is dependent on the state of another, even if they are far apart. This property allows quantum computers to perform computations that are impossible for classical computers.

4. Quantum Algorithms

Quantum algorithms, like **Shor's Algorithm** for factoring large numbers and **Grover's Algorithm** for search optimization, make use of quantum properties like superposition and entanglement to solve problems faster than classical computers.

Step 1: Choose Your Learning Platform

Several platforms now offer quantum computing environments where beginners can access quantum hardware and simulators. These platforms are designed to make quantum computing accessible without requiring expensive hardware or advanced knowledge of quantum mechanics. Here are some popular platforms to get you started:

1. IBM Q Experience

IBM Q Experience is one of the most popular platforms for learning quantum computing. It provides access to real quantum processors and simulators, allowing you to run quantum algorithms from anywhere with an internet connection. IBM offers a **quantum development environment** that includes tutorials, **Jupyter notebooks**, and access to real quantum hardware.

- **Getting Started on IBM Q Experience**:
    o Sign up for a free account on IBM Q Experience and gain access to their quantum computers and simulators.
    o Use the **Qiskit** library to write quantum programs in Python, and run them on IBM's quantum computers or simulators.

    o IBM also offers beginner-friendly tutorials to guide you through simple quantum programs, such as creating quantum circuits and understanding basic quantum algorithms.

2. Microsoft Quantum Development Kit (QDK)

Microsoft's QDK includes **Q#**, a high-level quantum programming language, and is supported by the **Quantum Development Environment**. Beginners can use Q# to write quantum algorithms and execute them on quantum simulators or hardware.

- **Getting Started on Microsoft QDK**:
    - o Download the Quantum Development Kit and start learning quantum programming using **Q#**.
    - o Microsoft also offers a collection of tutorials, documentation, and tools for building quantum applications.

3. Google's Cirq

Google's Cirq is an open-source quantum programming framework designed for writing, simulating, and running quantum algorithms on **quantum processors**. It is especially useful for research and development of quantum algorithms and supports various quantum hardware.

- **Getting Started on Cirq**:
  - o Install **Cirq** in your Python environment and begin writing quantum programs.
  - o Explore the **Google Quantum AI** website for learning resources and tutorials.

4. Rigetti Computing

Rigetti offers an integrated platform for quantum computing, including access to quantum hardware through the **Forest** suite and **quilc** (Quantum Instruction Language Compiler). They offer quantum simulators and tools for quantum software development.

- **Getting Started with Rigetti**:
  - o Sign up for an account and access their quantum processors and simulators.
  - o Learn how to write quantum programs using **Quil** (Quantum Instruction Language) and run them through the **Forest** platform.

Step 2: Learn Quantum Programming with Qiskit

If you choose IBM Q Experience, **Qiskit** is the quantum computing framework you will use to write and run quantum programs. Qiskit is a Python-based open-source library that allows you to create quantum circuits, execute them on simulators or real quantum hardware, and analyze the results.

Real-World Example: Writing Your First Quantum Program with Qiskit

1. **Install** **Qiskit**:
   To begin, you'll need to install **Qiskit** on your system. If you have Python installed, you can do this by running:

   ```bash
   bash
   ```

   ```bash
   pip install qiskit
   ```

2. **Create a Quantum Circuit**: Let's create a simple quantum circuit that applies a **Hadamard gate** to a qubit (which creates a superposition) and then measures the qubit.

   ```python
   python
   ```

   ```python
   from qiskit import QuantumCircuit, Aer, execute

   # Create a quantum circuit with one qubit
   qc = QuantumCircuit(1, 1)

   # Apply a Hadamard gate to the qubit
   (creates superposition)
   ```

235

```
qc.h(0)

# Measure the qubit and store the result in
classical bit 0
qc.measure(0, 0)

# Visualize the quantum circuit
print(qc)

# Use a simulator to execute the quantum
circuit
simulator                                   =
Aer.get_backend('qasm_simulator')

# Execute the circuit on the simulator
result     =     execute(qc,     simulator,
shots=1000).result()

# Get the results from the measurement
counts = result.get_counts(qc)
print("Measurement results:", counts)
```

3. **Run on Quantum Hardware**: Once you are comfortable with the basics, you can run the same quantum circuit on a real IBM quantum processor. In the Qiskit library, you can easily connect to IBM's quantum hardware via the IBM Q Experience interface.

```python
python
```

```python
from qiskit import IBMQ

# Load IBM Q account
IBMQ.load_account()

# Get the provider for accessing quantum
systems
provider = IBMQ.get_provider(hub='ibm-q')

# Choose a quantum system from the
available devices
backend                              =
provider.get_backend('ibmq_ourense')

# Execute the quantum circuit on the real
hardware
result    =    execute(qc,    backend,
shots=1000).result()

# Print the measurement results
counts = result.get_counts(qc)
print("Measurement        results        from
hardware:", counts)
```

Step 3: Explore Quantum Algorithms

Once you understand how to work with basic quantum circuits, you can start experimenting with **quantum algorithms**. Here are a few important algorithms you can try as a beginner:

1. Grover's Search Algorithm

Grover's algorithm is designed to find a specific item in an unsorted database faster than classical search algorithms.

2. Shor's Algorithm

Shor's algorithm solves the problem of factoring large numbers in polynomial time, which is exponentially faster than classical methods. It's especially important in breaking classical cryptographic systems like RSA.

3. Quantum Fourier Transform (QFT)

The Quantum Fourier Transform is a key component of many quantum algorithms, including Shor's algorithm, and provides a quantum version of the discrete Fourier transform.

4. Quantum Machine Learning

Quantum machine learning leverages quantum computers to speed up machine learning tasks, such as pattern recognition, classification, and optimization.

You can start exploring these algorithms through tutorials and resources available on platforms like **Qiskit** and **Microsoft's Quantum Development Kit**.

Step 4: Join Quantum Computing Communities

Quantum computing is an evolving field, and learning through communities can help you stay up to date with the latest developments and connect with other learners. Here are a few places to join the quantum community:

- **Qiskit Community**: IBM's Qiskit community provides a platform for discussion, tutorials, and sharing quantum projects.
- **Quantum Computing Stack Exchange**: A question-and-answer forum for quantum computing enthusiasts.
- **Quantum Open Source Foundation (QOSF)**: A community dedicated to the development of open-source quantum computing projects.

- **Meetups and Conferences**: Participate in **quantum meetups** and attend conferences like **Q2B** and **Quantum Computing Summit** to network and learn from industry experts.

Conclusion

Getting started with quantum computing may seem daunting, but with the right tools, platforms, and resources, anyone can begin learning and experimenting with this transformative technology. Platforms like **IBM Q Experience**, **Microsoft Quantum Development Kit**, and **Google Cirq** offer beginners access to quantum hardware and simulators, while libraries like **Qiskit** provide the tools necessary to write and execute quantum programs.

As you continue your journey in quantum computing, you'll be able to explore increasingly complex algorithms and applications that will play a crucial role in shaping the future of technology. Whether you're interested in **cloud computing**, **IoT**, **AI**, or **cryptography**, quantum computing offers endless possibilities for innovation and discovery.

In the next chapter, we will explore **quantum computing's potential in various industries**, focusing on how businesses and governments are preparing for the quantum future.

www.ingramcontent.com/pod-product-compliance
Lightning Source LLC
LaVergne TN
LVHW051320050326
832903LV00031B/3278